Oklahoma Series in Classical Culture

Echoes of Egyptian Voices

An Anthology of Ancient Egyptian Poetry

Translated by

John L. Foster

UNIVERSITY OF OKLAHOMA PRESS

Norman and London

Echoes of Egyptian Voices

By John L. Foster

Love Songs of the New Kingdom (New York, 1974)
*Thought Couplets and Clause Sequences in a Literary Text: The Maxims
of Ptah-Hotep* (Toronto, 1977)

This book is published with the generous assistance of The McCasland
Foundation, Duncan, Oklahoma.

We gratefully acknowledge permission to reprint the following:

"Leiden Hymn 20" first appeared in *Beloit Poetry Journal* 31 (Winter 1980–
81); "For a Portrait of the Queen in Luxor Temple" first appeared in *American Research Center in Egypt Newsletter* 81 (April 1972); "The Resurrection
of King Ounas" first appeared in "Some Observations on Pyramid Texts
273–274, the So-called 'Cannibal Hymn,'" *Journal of the Society for the Study
of Egyptian Antiquity* 9 (March 1979); "The Peasant's Eighth Complaint" first
appeared in *Bulletin of the Egyptological Seminar* 10 (1992).

Library of Congress Cataloging-in-Publication Data
Echoes of Egyptian voices : an anthology of ancient Egyptian poetry /
    [edited and] translated by John L. Foster.
        p.   cm. — (Oklahoma series in classical culture ; v. 12)
    Includes bibliographical references.
    ISBN 0-8061-2411-3
    1. Egyptian literature—Translations into English.   2. Egyptian
    poetry—Translations into English.   I. Foster, John L. (John
    Lawrence, 1930–   .   II. Series.
    PJ1943.E27   1992
    893'.1—dc20   91-50862
                                                             CIP

Text design by Bill Cason.

Echoes of Egyptian Voices: An Anthology of Ancient Egyptian Poetry is Volume 12
of the Oklahoma Series in Classical Culture.

The paper in this book meets the guidelines for permanence and durability
of the Committee on Production Guidelines for Book Longevity of the
Council on Library Resources, Inc. ∞

To
George R. Hughes
Opener of the Ways

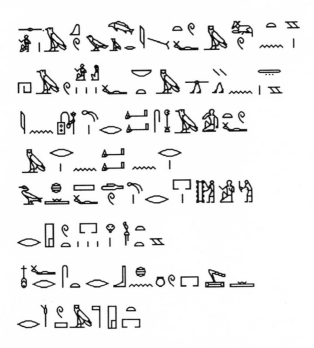

Man dies, his body is dust,
      his family all brought low to the earth;
But writing shall make him remembered,
      alive in the mouths of any who read.
Better a book than a builded mansion,
      better than body's home in the West,
Splendid above a fine house in the country
      or stone-carved deeds in the precinct of God.

Papyrus Chester Beatty IV
(ca. 1300–1100 B.C.)

Recto of the text of "Menna's Lament" (Oriental Institute Ostracon 12074. Courtesy of the Oriental Institute of The University of Chicago).

Contents

Preface

THE TWO GREAT hindrances to any proper appreciation of the literature and civilization of ancient Egypt are the Bible and the glory that was Greece. These two sources—and the civilizations that produced them—are the twin bastions of our Western culture; and since they have so undeniably formed us and the very ways we think, it is no wonder we approach other cultures in terms of what these two have taught us. Our view of ancient history is conditioned by what we understand as true from ancient Greece and, particularly, Israel. Indeed, our very idea of what constitutes ancient history is filtered through the accounts of Genesis and Exodus.

What has happened to Egyptology in the century and a half since Champollion deciphered the hieroglyphs, back at a time when one studied ancient Egypt only for confirmation of biblical attitudes? The difference has been the partial recovery, during the past 150 years, of the languages, histories, and cultures of the high civilizations of the ancient Near East, which enable us to study and understand a country like Egypt from its own documents and monuments, and from its own point of view. This increased knowledge demonstrates that the version of ancient history that we had accepted was very much oversimplified and parochial, projecting the viewpoint, at the earliest, of an ancient Israelite author during the united monarchy, some time after 1000 B.C. Egyptian writing, on the other hand, began some *two millennia* earlier, around 3000 B.C.; and civilization had been proceeding in high gear over the entire Fertile Crescent for at least that same two-thousand-year period before King David. We need to realize that some forty percent—*almost half*—of recorded human history occurred before King David. The selections in this volume are all from that earlier time, some of them from the earliest time, back toward the dawn of writing, of literature, and of history itself.

Because of our classical-Christian value system we have traditionally accepted the biblical account of ancient history as true and tried to fit evidence from extrabiblical sources into that system. This no longer works. Notice that the classical authorities, those upon whom the earliest students of ancient Egypt relied—Herodotus, Diodorus Siculus, and Strabo—were even later than the Yahwist and Elohist of Israelite tradition. Herodotus lived during the fifth century B.C.; and the others were both first-century figures. Even Manetho, from whom we take our division of Egyptian dynasties, lived only back as far as the third century B.C. Such writers—classical and Israelite alike—knew an Egypt that was but a shadow of its former self, that had long since ceded its greatness to later, more youthful empires.

There is another consequence of this unfortunate earlier perspective. Because we in the West have valued the contributions of the ancient Greeks and Hebrews as fundamental to our very being, we have lovingly preserved whatever was written in either language. Not too long ago a university education centered on a study of the Greek and Roman classics, and was often augmented by the study of Hebrew. The result has been over two millennia of careful attention to these ancient texts: the Hebrew because they were the sacred Word of God, and the Greek because they were the fountainhead of our Western literature and philosophy. Because of this high valuation, there has developed over the centuries a rich tradition of translating these relics of our origins. Translators can turn to the past to weigh how a passage was understood by many kindred spirits over time; and this slow process has improved and polished the results.

Now let us turn to the case of Egypt. Egyptian hieroglyphic is a dead language. Its meaning only began to be recovered when Champollion deciphered the hieroglyphs in 1822. And it was not until the last quarter of the nineteenth century that a tradition of translating the hieroglyphs into English could even begin to develop. Translation of ancient Egyptian literature is barely a century old; only four or five generations of Egyptologists have had a chance to work on the language; and most of the effort has of necessity been devoted to basics—vocabulary, word order, and sentence patterns. And these efforts of earlier language scholars have been absolutely fundamental to, and necessarily preceded, any attempt to recover ancient Egyptian literature as literature and as poetry.

Our very cultural traditions, along with loss of the key to the hieroglyphic language for so many centuries, have blinded us to the value of what has survived from the literature of ancient Egypt. It has riches thus far largely unrealized.

When one considers ancient Egypt, the first images that come to mind are of the pyramids at Giza, or the Sphinx, or the dried mummies in their coffins, or the consummate goldwork of the treasure of Tutankhamun, or the huge statues of Ramesses II. Egypt, indeed, was one of the first lights of civilization; and these images remind us of that fact. And when we ponder its surviving buildings and monuments, its carvings and paintings, its goldwork and jewelry, its statues and figurines, we cannot help but be impressed by its primacy. These survivals constitute the perennial fascination the world has with that ancient civilization. And as we look into the faces of Egyptian statues and figurines—which are usually generic and idealized, but lifelike—we wonder what went on in the minds of their owners, in the minds of those Egyptians the statues and figurines were meant to embody. We ask, what went on behind such eyes? What world did they see? What gave their faces their expressions?

Indeed, one wonders what a society that could create such excellence in architecture, in painting, in precious metal and stone, and in statuary—what did, or could, it similarly create in words? What Mind stood behind those hands that created the visual masterpieces of ancient Egypt? And how did that Mind express itself verbally? As one first trained in English and American literature, I have been intrigued by this aspect of Egyptian civilization for over twenty-five years. And I would argue that the splendor of pharaonic visual art has its worthy parallel in Egyptian literature: it is indeed a full-blooded verbal equivalent to the richness, elegance, vitality, and variety of Egypt's visual remains. Egyptians honored words as they became flesh in hymns and prayers, instructions, stories, and even love songs; and Egyptian writers—the poets particularly—delighted in working (or playing) with the nuances of words and meaning, and in the sounds and images of the language.

And yet the works of ancient Egyptian literature and their authors are less well known than the works of art and architecture. This is partly due to problems in deciphering the details of the language and partly to the condition of the surviving texts. But it is also due to the fact that it is easier to view the art and architecture of Egypt in pictures or on a tour than it is to read its literature, particularly for the nonspecialist. And in trying to read, one must also try to visualize the images and culture conveyed in the text—which is no easy thing to do. At any rate, far from appearing in their rightful place at the fountainhead of world literature, the classics of Egypt remain out of the mainstream and covered in darkness.

What can be said about that literature? First of all, the Egyptian language is old and venerable—known from the beginning of dynastic history (ca. 3100 B.C.) and lasting until the fourth century A.D., when the last hieroglyphic inscription was carved on the walls of the temple at Philae. By the time commemorative titles and tomb biographies become widespread during the Old Kingdom, we can see that a long history of the hieroglyphs had preceded them. Hieroglyphic signs at Saqqara from the tomb of King Djoser in the Third Dynasty (ca. 2630 B.C.) already show them in almost classic form. The ancient Egyptian language, then—from the unread earliest signs, through Old, Middle, and Late Egyptian, and on through Demotic and Coptic—had a documented career of almost 3,500 years. By contrast, English—as we can read it without too much aid—has so far survived for only 500 years (that is, back to Chaucer) and spans at best 1,000 years, if we go back to Anglo-Saxon, which must be studied as a foreign language. In addition to this long Egyptian time span, it is important to realize we have actual physical evidence from these very ancient historical periods: there are pot marks, incised kings' names, and inscriptions carved in stone, wood, and ivory that go back to the very earliest dynasties; papyri (which are extremely fragile) still survive, generally in fragments, some from the Old Kingdom; and ostraca (stones or potsherds with writing or drawing on them) are numerous from the New Kingdom and later. Egyptian literature is known to us, let us say, from originals. The text may not have been the author's hand copy; but it does come from the time when pharaonic Egypt was still vital, and often from the period in which the author wrote. We need not rely—as is the case, for instance, in biblical studies—on traditions only later written down or on several centuries of oral transmission.

During the past two decades much has been learned about the

nature of Egyptian literature. It was known all along that, as with the literatures of other ancient cultures, that of Egypt was almost exclusively religious. Ancient peoples seemed not to have atheism, agnosticism, or skepticism as options in the constellation of their beliefs. But it has now become apparent that ancient Egyptian literature is also almost entirely a verse literature. Very few of the compositions that we would term "literary" (i.e., *belles lettres*) were written in prose—perhaps some of the New Kingdom stories at best. Rather, all the primary genres—the didactic or "wisdom" texts (instructions, admonitions, and laments), the hymns and prayers, and most of the tales (fiction and myths)—were composed in verse.

The nature of this verse—the style of ancient Egyptian poetry—has also become clearer in recent years. The ancient Egyptian poet used a couplet form: the lines of his poems were grouped in twos, and each pair of lines completed a verse sentence. There were variations upon this basic form (triplets and quatrains); but the generalization is fundamental to understanding the structure of the poems. The verse line was clausal and syntactic: each line consisted of either a dependent or an independent clause; and the pair made up the full sentence. As I said before, the Egyptian poet loved to savor and play with words, since he so respected eloquence and fine language; and all the devices of major poetry were employed to enhance the poem: nuances in the vocabulary (connotations of words), imagery (the special images of the Nile Valley, of nature there, and of the various crafts, occupations, professions, and recreations of the people), figurative language (similes and metaphors occurred regularly to enrich meaning), and sound repetition (pervasively; for the Egyptian poet richness of sound harmonies was as important as collocations of ideas and images and symbols). In fact, ancient Egyptian poetry was most emphatically *not* a folk poetry (composed by splendidly intuitive untaught artists) but a sophisticated, artful court and temple poetry composed by authors skilled in a long tradition of the craft. The love of words was enriched by a similar love of all the devices used to enhance meaning and effect.

The major remaining gap in our knowledge of ancient Egyptian poetics concerns prosody. The ancient Egyptians did not write the vowels of their words; and since the language died out, these so far are lost to us. So we cannot for certain pronounce the language, even though we can understand and translate it. Because of the lack of vowels, and thus pronunciation, we are unable to scan the Egyptian verse line—we do not know for sure if it was composed of feet or of some freer means of determining accents and stresses. I myself would suggest the verse line was analogous to the free verse of Walt Whitman or the modernist American poets. In fact, I think the stylistic texture or flavor of ancient Egyptian poetry can best be described as a fusion of the free verse rhythms of those Americans just mentioned with the rhetorical and structural regularities—the strict attention to patterns of likeness and difference—of Alexander Pope's eighteenth-century heroic couplets (without the end rhyme or meter). This combination of stylistic and structural qualities I have termed the "thought couplet"; and the selections in this book are translated with that style and structure of Egyptian poetry in mind.

The wonder, however, is that we have any ancient Egyptian literature at all. The surfaces upon which the author wrote had to endure from two to five thousand years just so the text could physically survive the ravages of time. We are fortunate in two ways: many compositions were written on stone or pottery (which lasts better than, for instance, human bones); and the hot, dry climate of Egypt helps to preserve not only bones and other perishable objects, but papyrus, upon which many of the more valued texts were copied to keep them for their own day.

Even so, so much of ancient Egyptian literature is a matter of bits and tatters: ragged papyri with holes in them, crumbling into dust when handled, or splinters of stone and bits of pottery containing irritating and tantalizing fragments of text—keys that fail to unlock anything. Written in the margin of one papyrus we have, "When the wind comes, it veers toward the sycamore; / When you come . . ." And the rest is lost.

It is a long journey from the decaying fragments of stone and papyrus upon which ancient Egyptian literature is written to finished translations of that civilization's classics. Shown only the shattered pieces, one is bound to ask, with Ezekiel, Can these bones live? Can these bits and pieces, these hints of old poems written three and four thousand years ago, poems and stories and wisdom from the time of Moses and before, from before even Abraham, antedating his mythic wandering figure by centuries—can these fragments ever, through some miracle, come alive again to illuminate the thought and feeling—the consciousness—of their time, the days of their creators, showing us after so many centuries how men and women living in one of the first high civilizations—back at the very dawn of history and conscience—thought, felt, and acted—how the human mind worked so long ago? Can not only the letter but the spirit of the words they wrote be resurrected?

The answer, I think—admitting that the journey from stone to poem is dotted with pitfalls and that recovering Mind is much chancier than recovering stones and potsherds—is, largely, yes. We *can* "come upon the ancient people" (as Ezra Pound tried to do in his *Cantos* for over half a century, "to gather from the air a live tradition"); we *can* recover to a good degree the consciousness behind the shattered remnants of the words and literature of a great and enduring civilization. While so often the texts, as we now have them, are fragmentary, many are, or can be made, almost or entirely complete; we *can* determine a hieroglyphic text upon which to base a translation; and we *do* know enough of the Egyptian language—its grammar, vocabulary, clause structure, and, for poetry especially, its style—to derive a believable English translation from the original.

How do we proceed? If a complete text is available, say, on a clean, untattered, neatly written papyrus, then one proceeds directly to transcribing the hieratic handwriting into hieroglyphs; and from there, one begins a literal translation of the text into English. But much Egyptian literature must be reconstructed; it must be slowly and painstakingly put together from small pieces. The process is analogous to completing a jigsaw puzzle—with the added complication that for the same final picture we have pieces from different copies, all cut differently and all in the same horrendous pile to be sorted out and made sense of. And usually we have too many pieces that fit in one part, overlapping and confusing each other, while there are all too often pieces missing from other parts.

If the scholar is fortunate enough to possess multiple versions of a text, these are lined up in parallel with each other so that like sentences and passages in each version appear together for comparison. In this manner the quality of each version can be ascertained and an "eclectic" text developed—a single final text composed of the best readings from all the individual versions. Only then is the piece ready for translation.

This stage too is often a laborious one. Here the scholar aims at what is called a "literal" translation, transforming the hieroglyphs into English more or less on a word-for-word basis. There is some difference of opinion as to just how free such a translation should be; and my own practice has usually been to keep to the word-for-word version generally, preserving most of the Egyptian order of words and clauses, so that the next scholar can follow the choices I have made in the transfer from one language to another. This literal translation is the most important single stage of the progress from broken stone to final poem. Unfortunately, at this stage there is also no poem. The literal translation has not, and should not pretend to have, any literary value. Lovers of literature and poetry in English would recoil in horror at the butchery done to the language in many such translations. A late colleague has characterized this idiom of the scholarly literal as "King-James-ese," for its failed attempt to re-create the stately and antique atmosphere of the A.D. 1611 translation of the English Bible.

With the literal translation, then, we have only a skeleton of meaning—they are still dry bones, with no flesh upon them and no breath of life breathed into them. The text is still the document of the philologist and not yet the living creature of the poet, with, as is often said in literary studies, an independent life of its own—since the masterwork outlives its creator. How does one go that last stage of the journey? How to move from literal to literary? How to transmute a "text" into a "poem"?

In this final stage the translator must shift his or her value system from that of the scholar—cautious, meticulous, analytic, skeptical, scientific—to that of the poet—spontaneous, synthetic, imaginative, emotional, and whatever other qualities you may wish to attribute to the creative artist. For the translator-poet, of course, there is a text to begin with whose words and literal meaning must be respected, or one tends to create new poems but not poetic translations of meaning from another language.

And what interests the poet-translator in that literal text are the same facts and qualities we seek in reading modern poems. We want to know who is speaking the poem, who the characters are, where the situation takes place, and what goes on. We also want to know the thoughts and feelings of the persons in the poem, their attitudes and emotions. And we look for words well placed and things excellently said; that is, we also look for quality in the poet's use of tools, and we thus want excellence of workmanship and style. In a word, we want to be treated to a single, unified, compelling moment (or series of moments) of human experience. And for an Egyptian poem translated into English, that means an attempt to recover patches of human experience from three and four thousand years ago. The speakers of these poems must stand alive before us once again to show us why that now anonymous Egyptian poet wanted to put his time and people into words. In this way, the life of an exile, Sinuhe, in the pharaonic Egypt of the twentieth century B.C., can be recovered to enrich the lives of those in the twentieth century A.D.

So, as the translator-poet works on the texts, he or she looks for the incident or emotion or mood that seems to have inspired the original poem, from which it all grew in the Egyptian poet's imagination. And the translator looks for images, turns of phrase, and connotations attached to the literal words, listening in order, as Dylan Thomas once said, "to hear words whispering to one another." And it is from such elements, and from the recreative imagination, that the modern translator revivifies the poem: it becomes the *text transfigured*. And if the translator is lucky, and talented, experienced in the original language, and has worked hard at the craft of words in English, then, perhaps, the result is a poem that can delight and even illumine the modern reader or hearer. The literal translation communicates only one of the kinds of meaning, the "intellectual." But there are other kinds—emotional meaning, imaginative meaning, the meaning conveyed by tone, images, metaphors, and symbols, all of which contribute to the multidimensional language of poetry. In the literary translation these other kinds of meaning are included; more is attempted, and when successful, more is recovered from the dustheaps of the past.

What is the rightful place of ancient Egyptian literature in world literature? Along with the Sumero-Akkadian literature, it is the world's first—the earliest expression of humankind's experiences and hopes and dreams, of the human encounter with nature and the gods, with other persons, with people of other nations (sometimes hostile), with daily life, with miracles, with the ups and downs of society and politics, and with our inner, sometimes turbulent or bewildered, self. It is, even now, a rich literature, despite the fact that it lies before us in ruins. Enough remains for us to insist flatly that its masterpieces belong at the beginning of our traditions of world literature—as the fountainhead, preceding the contributions of Greece and Israel. There is an entire era of our human venture, lasting approximately two millennia, that produced sometimes brilliant literary pieces; and of this era we know very little. Fascinated as we are by pyramids and mummies, we know almost nothing of Egypt's verbal heritage. Yet that inheritance is ours also; and we have been too long blinded by our own formative traditions to the older, sometimes deeper, and now alien excellence of Egypt and the other high cultures of the ancient Near East.

Finally, all translators worthy of their salt want, with Pound, to "make it new" for their own time and language. Yet, in closing, I also want to stress that these translations are meant to be a critical reading of the ancient Egyptian poetic texts in the original—a reading that Egyptologists too, I trust, can address with profit. The poems result from an affection for the culture, people, language, and poetry of ancient Egypt that is of many years' standing; and my intent is that these echoes of the ancient voices ring true.

JOHN L. FOSTER

Evanston, Illinois

Acknowledgments

I WANT TO express my gratitude to the National Endowment for the Humanities for fellowships in 1971 and 1983, and to my own institution, Roosevelt University, for research fellowships in 1973, 1987, and 1991, all of which helped me in major ways to pursue the study and translation of ancient Egyptian literature. I am also grateful to the American Research Center in Egypt and the Society for the Study of Egyptian Antiquities for providing a forum in their annual meetings where many of the poems were first read and discussed. I also want to thank Barbara Siegemund-Broka of the University of Oklahoma Press for a thorough job of editing my manuscript; her questions and suggestions have made this a better book. Finally, I want to thank Michael Berger, whose copyrighted hieroglyphic font, *Proglyph*, I have used to construct the Egyptian texts in the epigraph and conclusion of this book.

But my greatest debt is to Gloria, Ann, Kristen, and Robert. May they live, prosper, and be happy.

Echoes of Egyptian Voices

The Instruction for Merikare

T HIS INSTRUCTION was composed during the earlier twenty-first century B.C. probably by King Khety of Dynasty X for his son Merikare. The following hymn to the Creator God is an early gem of ancient Egyptian literature, showing God as preeminent among the gods, hidden, caring, one who created the universe for all human beings, and who created humankind in his own image. The universe, the author also insists, is founded upon justice.

The generations come and go among mankind,
    and God, who knows all natures, still lies hidden.
None lift a hand against the powerful,
    and everywhere the eye sees ruin;
One worships whatever god is met upon the way
    made of enduring stone or born from metal.
And yet the thirsty reservoirs are filled with waters of the flood,
    nor is there river yet that can conceal him,
And it is he who frees the stopped canal,
    for in such ways his veiled Spirit moves.

The gone soul journeys on to whence it came,
    nor can it ever stray to paths of yesteryear.
So, "Make your home fine in the West," they said,
    "raise high your seat in the realm under God"—
But through care in accomplishing Justice!
    The hearts of the very gods lean on Justice:
Esteemed are the gestures of the upright heart
    more than the gift-ox of one who does wrong.
Act so toward God that he act thus toward you.
    But rich provisions, they only green altars;

What conduct carves, thence your good name.
    And God well knows who serves him.

Provide for mankind, the flock of God,
    for he made earth and heaven for their sake;
He soothed the raging darkness of primeval waters,
    and he created heart's breath that they might have life.
They are his living images, come from his very self,
    that he might shine forth in the heavens upon them.
And he created for them plants and foliage,
    and small beasts, fowl, and fishes were their food.
Yet he destroyed his enemies, diminished his own children,
    when they, ungrateful, planned revolt against him.

For their sake he created light
    that he might sail about the sky to see them;
He wove a holy dwelling round about them:
    and when they weep, he hears.
He created for them godly rulers from the womb,
    leaders to fortify the backbones of the weak;
He gave them supernatural power to be a weapon
    and to counteract the blows of fate.

Watch over them, by night as well as day.
    God has struck down the rebel hearts among them
Much as a father disciplines his son to ease his brother.
    And God knows every name.

4

Akhenaten's Hymn to the Sun

OMPOSED CIRCA 1350 B.C., possibly by King Akhenaten himself (who is the speaker of the poem), this hymn exalts the one God who created heaven and earth—but here in his visible (not hidden) form as the Sun, which makes all life possible. The poet's loving emphasis upon nature and God's creatures and upon the beauty and variety of creation is obvious. Akhenaten is presented as the bodily Son of God and intercedes with him for humankind.

I

Let your holy Light shine from the height of heaven,
    O living Aten,
        source of all life!
From eastern horizon risen and streaming,
    you have flooded the world with your beauty.
You are majestic, awesome, bedazzling, exalted,
        overlord over all earth,
    yet your rays, they touch lightly, compass the lands
        to the limits of all your creation.
There in the Sun, you reach to the farthest of those
    you would gather in for your Son,
        whom you love;
Though you are far, your light is wide upon earth;
    and you shine in the faces of all
        who turn to follow your journeying.

II

When you sink to rest below western horizon,
    earth lies in darkness like death,

Sleepers are still in bedchambers, heads veiled,
      eye cannot spy a companion;
All their goods could be stolen away,
      heads heavy there, and they never knowing!
Lions come out from the deeps of their caves,
      snakes bite and sting;
Darkness muffles, and earth is silent:
      he who created all things lies low in his tomb.

III

Earth-dawning mounts the horizon,
      glows in the sun-disk as day:
You drive away darkness, offer your arrows of shining,
      and the Two Lands are lively with morningsong.
Sun's children awaken and stand,
      for you, golden light, have upraised the sleepers;
Bathed are their bodies, who dress in clean linen,
      their arms held high to praise your Return.
Across the face of the earth
      they go to their crafts and professions.

IV

The herds are at peace in their pastures,
      trees and the vegetation grow green;
Birds start from their nests,
      wings wide spread to worship your Person;
Small beasts frisk and gambol, and all
      who mount into flight or settle to rest
            live, once you have shone upon them;
Ships float downstream or sail for the south,
      each path lies open because of your rising;
Fish in the River leap in your sight,
      and your rays strike deep in the Great Green Sea.

V

It is you create the new creature in Woman,
      shape the life-giving drops into Man,
Foster the son in the womb of his mother,
      soothe him, ending his tears;
Nurse through the long generations of women
                        to those given Air,
      you ensure that your handiwork prosper.
When the new one descends from the womb
      to draw breath the day of his birth,
You open his mouth, you shape his nature,
      and you supply all his necessities.

VI

Hark to the chick in the egg,
      he who speaks in the shell!
   You give him air within
      to save and prosper him;
And you have allotted to him his set time
      before the shell shall be broken;
Then out from the egg he comes,
      from the egg to peep at his natal hour!
   and up on his own two feet goes he
      when at last he struts forth therefrom.

VII

How various is the world you have created,
      each thing mysterious, sacred to sight,
O sole God,
      beside whom is no other!
You fashioned earth to your heart's desire,
      while you were still alone,
Filled it with man and the family of creatures,
      each kind on the ground, those who go upon feet,
      he on high soaring on wings,

The far lands of Khor and Kush,
and the rich Black Land of Egypt.

VIII

And you place each one in his proper station,
where you minister to his needs;
Each has his portion of food,
and the years of life are reckoned him.
Tongues are divided by words,
natures made diverse as well,
Even men's skins are different
that you might distinguish the nations.

IX

You make Hapy, the Nile, stream through the underworld,
and bring him, with whatever fullness you will,
To preserve and nourish the People
in the same skilled way you fashion them.
You are Lord of each one,
who wearies himself in their service,
Yet Lord of all earth, who shines for them all,
Sun-disk of day, holy Light!
All of the far foreign countries—
you are the cause they live,
For you have put a Nile in the sky
that he might descend upon them in rain—
He makes waves on the very mountains
like waves on the Great Green Sea
to water their fields and their villages.

X

How splendidly ordered are they,
your purposes for this world,
O Lord of eternity, Hapy in heaven!
Although you belong to the distant peoples,
to the small shy beasts

who travel the deserts and uplands,
Yet Hapy, he comes from Below
        for the dear Land of Egypt as well.
And your Sunlight nurses each field and meadow:
    when you shine, they live,
        they grow sturdy and prosper through you.
You set seasons to let the world flower and flourish—
    winter to rest and refresh it,
        the hot blast of summer to ripen;
And you have made heaven far off
    in order to shine down therefrom,
        in order to watch over all your creation.

XI

You are the one God,
    shining forth from your possible incarnations
        as Aten, the Living Sun,
Revealed like a king in glory, risen in light,
    now distant, now bending nearby.
You create the numberless things of this world
        from yourself, who are One alone—
    cities, towns, fields, the roadway, the River;
And each eye looks back and beholds you
    to learn from the day's light perfection.
O God, you are in the Sun-disk of Day,
    Over-Seer of all creation
        —your legacy
        passed on to all who shall ever be;
For you fashioned their sight, who perceive your universe,
    that they praise with one voice
            all your labors.

XII

And you are in my heart;
    there is no other who truly knows you
        but for your son, Akhenaten.

May you make him wise with your inmost counsels,
> wise with your power,
>> that earth may aspire to your godhead,
>>> its creatures fine as the day you made them.
Once you rose into shining, they lived;
>> when you sink to rest, they shall die.
For it is you who are Time itself,
>> the span of the world;
>>> life is by means of you.

Eyes are filled with beauty
>>> until you go to your rest;
All work is laid aside
>>> as you sink down the western horizon.

Then, Shine reborn!   Rise splendidly!
>> my Lord, let life thrive for the King
Who has kept pace with your every footstep
>>> since you first measured ground for the world.
Lift up the creatures of earth for your Son
>>> who came forth from your Body of Fire!

The Debate Between a Man Tired of Life and His Soul

T HE FOLLOWING poem is a discussion—at times acrimonious—
between a man so dispirited he wants to die and his *ba*, or soul,
which insists that one must endure life until the end comes natu-
rally. The single surviving papyrus, its beginning lost, dates to
Dynasty XII, about 2000–1800 B.C. It is a profound text and difficult to
translate. Yet the man's despair gives rise to some of the finest lyric poetry to
survive from ancient Egypt.

I

. . . .

[*The man's* ba-*bird, or soul, is concluding a speech:*]

. . . .

"The tongues of the gods, they do not speak amiss,
    they make no special cases."

I I

I opened my mouth to my soul
    that I might answer what it had said:

"This is more than I can bear just now!
    —my soul could find no time for me!
It is beyond belief
    —as if I should hesitate to do the deed!
Let my soul not disappear like this, not flutter off,
    but let it take its stand beside me—
Or never shall it have the chance
    to wrap my person in its stifling bonds;
And for all its twitter, never
    shall it escape the Day of Reckoning.

11

"O all you gods,
　　　　see how my soul defames me!
I will not listen to it ever
　　　　as I drag my way toward dissolution;
For it will not help me do the death by fire—
　　　　myself the victim, who shall no more suffer.

"Let it be near me on the Day of Reckoning!
　　　　Let it stand tall on that side yonder
　　　　　　as one who shares my joy!
Yet this the very soul that rushes off, it vanishes,
　　　　to separate itself from death.
My foolish soul is going to ease the pains of living, is it?
　　　　Keep me from death until I come to it by nature?

"No! make the West sweet for me now!
　　　　Is there not pain and suffering enough?
—That is the stuff of life: a troubled journey, a circuit of the sun;
　　　　even the trees decay and fall.

"O tread you down upon injustice,
　　　　end my helplessness!
Judge me, O Thoth, you who can soothe the gods;
　　　　defend, O Khonsu, me, a teller of the truth;
Hear, O Re, my speaking, you who command the skyship;
　　　　defend me, O Anubis, in the holy hall of judgment—
Because my need is heavy in the scale,
　　　　and it has raised the pan of sweetness out of reach.
　　　　　　　　Preserve, O gods, the quiet center of my being!"

III

What my soul said to me:

"You are no man at all!
　　　　Are you even alive?
How full you are of your complaints of life

like a man of means preaching to passersby!
Things sink down to ruin. Well, save yourself by getting up!
        There are no bonds on you as of some prisoner whining,
'I shall get even with you:
        and you, your name shall die!
Life! That is the place of fluttering down,
        heart's own desire, the district of the West
            . . . after a troubled crossing.'"

I V

[*I continued:*]

"If my soul, my foolish brother, would only listen,
        its wish would be like mine;
And it would perch most blest at my right hand,
        reaching the West like one who has a pyramid
            towering for after-generations over his grave.

"And I would wave the sacred fan above your listless form
        that you attract another soul to join you, weary one;
And I would wave the fan again, then say the spell,
        so you might lure a different, fiery soul;
I would find drink from inshore eddies, raise up food,
        beguile some other hungry soul to stay with you.
But if you keep me back from death this way,
        I promise you no peace in the West forever!

"Be still, my soul, my brother,
        until a successor comes with offerings
To stand at the tomb on burial day
        and deck a bed in the city of God."

V

Then my soul opened its mouth to me
        that it might answer what I had said:

13

"Your graveyard thoughts bring sadness to the heart,
        and tears, feeding our misery;
That is what shovels a man into his house
        dug in the rock on the high hill:
There, there is no more coming forth for you
        to see the sunny days,
Or workmen crafting their buildings in granite,
        putting last touches on pyramids,
Or the beauties of the monuments,
        or where builders fashion altars for the gods:
You are emptied and drear, like those without motion
        dead on the riverbank, no one caring:
Water laps at their backs,
        the sun does its work,
                and, lips in the current, fish whisper to them.

"Now listen to me—
        pay some attention to what people say:
                Spend your days happily! Forget your troubles!

"There was a man, and he farmed his plot of land;
        and he was loading his harvest into a ship
                for the voyage to his accounting, which drew near.
And he saw coming a night of wind and weather
        so that he was watchful of the ship, waiting for day,
While he dreamed of life with his wife and children
        who had perished on the Lake of Death
                on a dark night, with crocodiles.
And after he was pondering there some time,
        he shaped the silence into words, saying,
'I have not wept that mother yonder—
        for her there is no returning from the West,
                no more than any who have lived on earth.
But let me mourn the children, killed in her womb,
        who saw the face of Death ere ever they were born.'

"There was another man, and he wanted his evening meat;
    and there was his wife, saying,
       'There will be bread.'
And he went outdoors to fume awhile
    and then go back inside
Behaving like a better person
    (his wife was wise to his ways).
Yet he never really listened to her,
       so the death demons came and carried him off."

V I

I opened my mouth to my soul
    that I might answer what it had said:

i

"How my name stinks because of you
    more than the stink of bird dung on a summer's day
       under a burning sky.
How my name stinks because of you
    more than the catch of fish on a good angling day
       under a burning sky.
How my name stinks because of you
    more than the stench of marsh birds on the hummocks
       filthy with waterfowl.
How my name stinks because of you
    more than the fishermen's smell at runnels of swamps
       after they have been fishing.
How my name stinks because of you
    more than the reek of crocodiles sunning on sandbanks
       alive with their crocodile kind.
How my name stinks because of you
    more than the wife about whom lies
       are told to her wedded husband.
How my name stinks because of you
    more than the able youth of whom they falsely say
       that he is prisoner of everything he should despise.

15

How my name stinks because of you
> more than the crocodile's cove, where the fool taunts him
> careful his back is turned.

i i

"Who is there to talk to today?
> Brothers are evil;
>> the friends of today, they do not love us.

Who is there to talk to today?
> Hearts are rapacious;
>> each man covets his neighbor's goods.

Who is there to talk to today?
> Gentleness is dead;
>> brute strength bears down on everyone.

Who is there to talk to today?
> Men are proud of the evil they do;
>> good everywhere falls defeated.

Who is there to talk to today?
> A man is maddened by evil fortune;
>> the sad injustice moves all to laughter.

Who is there to talk to today?
> Robbery, plundering;
>> each man a predator on his companion.

Who is there to talk to today?
> The malefactor masks as best friend;
>> the trusted brother turns into an enemy.

Who is there to talk to today?
> There is no thought for tradition;
>> no one nurturing decency these days.

Who is there to talk to today?
> Brother betray;
>> they take to strangers, not men of integrity.

Who is there to talk to today?
> Faces are wiped out;
>> each, high or low, fighting all others.

Who is there to talk to today?
> Hearts are selfish and slick;

no heart to lean on.
Who is there to talk to today?
    There are no righteous men;
        earth is abandoned to evil.
Who is there to talk to today?
    Emptiness in trusted friends;
        blind ignorance to life that brings wisdom.
Who is there to talk to today?
    No man of satisfied mind;
        one to walk quietly with does not exist.
Who is there to talk to today?
    I am bowed too low with my misery
        lacking someone to share the thoughts in my heart.
Who is there to talk to today?
    Wrongdoing beats on the earth,
        and of it there is no end.

i i i

"So death is before me now—
    the healthy state of sick man—
        like coming out in the air after suffering.
So death is before me now
    like the fragrance of myrrh
        or sailing at ease on a breezy day.
So death is before me now
    like aroma of flowers,
        like being drunk in a promised land.
So death is before me now
    like the breath of a new Inundation,
        like coming home from a long expedition.
So death is before me now
    like a clearing sky,
        like understanding what perplexed us before.
So death is before me now
    like one longing to see his home
        after long years in prison.

"But to be one who is over there
        with living God
                fighting evil for Him who made him!
But to be one who is over there
        erect in the skyship
                offering choice gifts to the temples!
But to be one who is over there!
        One who finally, perfectly knows!
                And he shall never be kept from approaching

                                                great God

                whenever he would speak!"

VII

What my soul said to me:

        "Put your murmuring aside now.

"O you who belong to me, my brother,
        must you be sacrifice upon the flaming altar?
Friend, fight on the side of life!
        Say to me, 'Love me *here!*'
Put thoughts of the West behind you!
        Love! yes, love, indeed,
So that you may in due time reach the West,
        may touch your body gently to the earth;
And I shall flutter down beside you
        when you are weary of the world at last.
                Then shall we two be fellow citizens together."

The Resurrection of King Ounas

T HIS VERY ancient hymn—from about 2300 B.C., and thus toward
the beginning of surviving Egyptian literature—can still be seen
carved on the wall of the burial chamber of King Ounas of Dynasty V in the Old Kingdom. It commemorates the death of the
king—or, better, his transfiguration from inert body to active power in his
true home among the gods. The author envisions a communion feast in
which lesser gods are hunted down, butchered and boiled, and then eaten
by the king so as to neutralize their power and so that their essence will
revive and nourish him and enhance his power. There is no evidence for
cannibalism during historic times in Egypt; and such a religious ceremony—
even if it took place only in the author's imagination—indicates very ancient roots for the poem.

I

A pale sky darkens,
   stars hide away,
Nations of heavenly bowmen are shaken,
   bones of the earth-gods tremble—
All cease motion, are still,
   for they have looked upon OUNAS, the King,
Whose Soul rises in glory, transfigured, a god,
   alive among his fathers of old time,
     nourished by ancient mothers.

I I

The King, this is he! Lord of the twisty ways of wisdom
   (whose very mother knew not his name),
His magnificence lights the black sky,
   his power flames in the Land of the Risen—

19

Like Atum his father, who bore him;
     and once having born him,
          strong was the Son more than the Father!
The *kas* of the King hover about him;
     feminine spirits steady his feet;
Familiar gods hang over him;
     uraei rear from his brow;
And his guiding Serpent precedes:
     "Watch over the Soul!
          Be helpful, O Fiery One!"
All the Mighty Companions are guarding the King!

III

The King, this is he! strong Bull of the Sky
     with blood-lust in his heart,
Who feasts on the incarnation of each god,
     eating the organs of those
Who come, their bodies fat with magical power,
     fresh from the Isle of Flame.

IV

The King, this is he! his Change now accomplished,
     united again with his blessed Spirits.
The King is arisen, transfigured, become this great God,
     lord over acolyte gods;
He sits
     and his back is toward earth.

V

The King, this is he! who deals out judgment
     sitting in concert with One
          (whose Name must ever be hidden)
     this day when sacrifice comes to the firstborn.

The King, this is he! lord of the offering meal,
    he knots the sacred cord,
        provides his own gifts for the altar.

The King, this is he! who eats men,
    feeds upon gods;
Keeper of tribute victims,
    he renders swift sentence.

V I

It is Seizer of Scalp-locks who ropes them in for the King;
    He of the Upreared Head it is hobbles them,
        dragging them near for him;
The Chief over Blood Rites binds them,
    and Traveler throws down the Lords-god
That he might cut their throats for the King,
    cut from their bodies what is inside them—
This is the envoy of judgment he sends
    to deal execution.
And then the Bloody-Eyed butchers them,
    cooks the pieces of them for the King,
        filling his kettles at dinnertime.

V I I

The King, this is he! who eats down their magic,
    swallows their vital power.
Their biggest belong to his meal at daybreak;
    those in between are for dinner;
Their smallest are his provisions at nightfall;
    and their old men and women?
        —sticks for his hearthstones!

Great gods of the northern heaven lay fire to his stew-pots—
    their contents the thighs of the firstborn.
Sky-dwellers fly about serving the King,
    stirring his kettles with legs of their women.

They travel throughout the Twin Heavens for him,
    they people the world's Two Shores.

VIII

The King, this is he! a great Power,
    potent among the all-Powerful!

The King, this is he! hawk-image of the divine,
    best likeness among fierce forms of the Great One
        —hungriest of the hunters:
Any he finds in his way,
    he eats him down bit by bit.
Oh, the King's proper seat is surely as Chief,
    before the ranked Great in the Land of Glory!

The King, this is he! a god,
    older than eldest;
Thousands go about serving him,
    hundreds there are heap his offering tables.

There has been given him witness and warrant:
    "This one is one of the Great Gods!"
        thus says Orion, ancestral father.

IX

The King has risen again, translated to heaven;
    and the Bodily Form shines forth,
        Lord of the Land of the Glorified!
He has shattered the bones of the vertebrae,
    seized on the hearts of the gods;
He has dined upon blood,
    swallowed down the fresh pieces,
To be nourished by lungs of the wise ones,
    to be warmed with life from their hearts
        and their magic power as well.

Upraised is the King (look, he rises!)
　　to feast on the bits afloat in the red broth!
And the Bodily Form, it stirs! it quickens!
　　their magic is working within him!
Nevermore can his heavenly glory be gone from him:
　　he has taken unto himself
　　　　the genius of every god.

X

The time of the King now, it is eternity,
　　his boundaries, they touch infinity,
Through this his power to do what he will,
　　avoid whatever he hates,
　　　　concerning all things in the kingdom of heaven
　　　　　　throughout all space and time.

X I

So now, their souls are at home within the King's body,
　　their turbulent energy under his spell,
Through this his communion consisting of gods,
　　boiled for the King from their bones.

So now, their souls are the King's subjects,
　　and the ghosts are gone from their broken forms.
The King is free from all these!
　　Risen!　Arisen!
　　Lasting!　Everlasting!
NEVERMORE shall the power of deities be deadly
　　who would hack the abode where the heart of OUNAS
　　　　dwells 'mid the living on this our earth
　　　　　　for ever and ever more.

The Tale of the Shipwrecked Sailor

T HE FOLLOWING story from the twentieth century B.C. is a tall tale or sailor's yarn—of shipwreck, a magic desert island, and a lordly talking snake. It is told in a seemingly simple and artless manner, as befits a fairy tale. Yet the charm of the narration comes from the constant touches of humor, comedy, and irony, which confirm that the author was a skilled composer of such narratives. The main story is framed by hints of another, just visible in the presence of the "leader" at its beginning and end. The sailor himself is a comic character—assertive, blustery, overconfident, forgetful of past favors, and unaware of the ironies of his speech and situation; and with the serpent's narration we actually have a tale within a tale within a tale.

The following was told by a master teller:

Be hale of heart, my leader!
    Look, we have come through!
The mallet has been taken, the mooring peg struck in,
    the forward rope secured upon the land;
Thanksgiving has been offered, god is praised,
    each man embraces his companion.
Your crew has come back safely,
    there are no losses to our expedition
Though we traversed the northern marches of Wawat
    and skirted Senmut fortress.
Just look at us, we are successfully returned—
    this is our country; we are home!

Now, hear me out, my leader;
    I am a man who never stretches truth:

Purify yourself, pour water on your fingers!
       Thereafter you can answer what is put to you
That you address the King staunch-hearted,
       responding with no hesitation.
The mouth of a man can save him;
       speech can soften an angry face. . . .

       —Well, never mind.
You do whatever in the world you want, then;
       it gets to be a bother, talking to you!

But let me tell you just a little story, a bit like this,
       which happened once upon a time to me.
I was traveling to the region of the royal mines
       and had descended to the Great Green Sea
In a grand two-hundred-foot-long vessel
       (its width was seventy feet from rail to rail),
The crew within it, one hundred twenty
       of the finest men in Egypt:
Let them see only sky, let them see land,
       braver were their hearts than lions;
They could foretell a storm before its coming,
       foul weather before ever it occurred.

A storm came up—with us on the open sea—
       and no chance for us to reach harbor;
The wind grew sharp and made a constant moaning,
       and there were hungry fourteen-foot-high waves!
A piece of wood of some sort hit me,
       and then the ship was dead.
           Of all those fine men, not a one survived.

Then I was carried to a desert island
       by a swell of the Great Green Sea.
I spent three days alone,
       my heart my sole companion;

I nested in the shelter of a covering tree
     and hugged the shadows.
Finally, I stretched my legs
     in order to discover what to eat;
And I found figs and grapes there
     and every sort of tasty greens,
And sycamore figs, and notched figs,
     and cucumbers that looked cared for,
And fish, and birds—
     there was nothing that that island did not have!
Then I filled myself past satisfaction,
     spilling and dropping the abundance in my arms.
I shaped a fire drill, and made a fire,
     and gave burnt offering to the gods.

Then I heard a sound as of approaching storm,
     and I assumed it was another Great Green Sea wave—
          trees were breaking, ground was quaking—
I bared my face
     and found it was a serpent coming my way:
The thing was over fifty huge feet long!
     its beard hung down a yard,
Its flesh was gilt,
     its eyebrows lapis lazuli;
          and it reared up in front.

It bared its mouth at me—
     I lying prone in fear and trembling—
     and spoke:
"What brings you? brings you?
     Little man, what brings you?
If you delay to tell me
     what brings you to this isle,
I promise that you shortly shall be ashes—
     become like something that has never been."

"Though you just spoke to me,
  I am not all quite here to hear it;
I am, I know, before you
  but hardly know myself."

Then he put me in his mouth
  and took me to his place of residence
And set me down again without ill-treatment:
  I still was whole—no bites were out of me.
He bared his mouth once more,
  I on my belly on the ground before him,
    and said:
"What brings you? brings you?
  Little man, what brings you
To this island of the Great Green Sea
  with shores as changing as the shifty waves?"

This time I told him all about it,
  my arms raised humbly in his presence,
    saying:
"I was traveling to the region of the royal mines
  on an errand of the King
In a grand two-hundred-foot-long vessel
  (its width was seventy feet from rail to rail),
The crew within it, one hundred twenty
  of the finest men in Egypt:
Let them see only sky, let them see land,
  braver were their hearts than lions;
They could foretell a storm before its coming,
  foul weather before ever it occurred.
Each in his heart was steadier,
  his arm more powerful, than his companion—
    there was no sluggard in the lot!

"A storm came up—with us on the open sea—
  and no chance for us to reach harbor;

The wind grew sharp and made a constant moaning,
      and there were hungry fourteen-foot-high waves!
A piece of wood of some sort hit me,
      and then the ship was dead.
Of those fine men, not one survived, except for me—
      see, down here, beside you.
Then I was carried to this desert island
      by a swell of the Great Green Sea."

Then he said to me,
      "Fear not, fear not!
My little man, you must not pale your face so—
      you have reached me!
Look, God has let you live
      that he might bring you to this phantom isle.
There is nothing that it does not have,
      it is full of every fine and lovely thing!

"Now, you are going to spend one month, and then another,
      until you finish four months on this island.
Then a ship will come from Egypt
      with sailors in it whom you know
That you may go with them toward home
      and die in your own city.
What joy for one who lives to tell the things he has been through
      when the suffering is over!

"But let me tell you just a little story, a bit like yours,
      which happened on this very isle while I was here
            living with companions and my children
                  in one great extended family.
We totaled five and seventy persons,
      consisting of my offspring, relatives, and friends
(I cannot bear to dwell on a small daughter
      brought to me through prayer):

"A star fell
        and they were gone, gone up in flame.
It happened when I could not be there . . . all burned . . .
        and I not even with them.
I wanted to be dead instead of them
        after finding them a heap of tangled corpses.

"If you have courage, steel your heart
        that you may fill your arms with children,
And kiss your wife,
        and see your home.
Believe me, it is better than all else
        when you are back again
                and dwell within the bosom of your friends."

Now I was lying stretched out on the ground,
        and I touched head to earth before him in respect:
"Let me say something to you:
        let me chronicle your glories for my King,
                cause him to be acquainted with your highness;
Let me arrange to have them bring you precious ointments,
        balsam, spices, perfumes, sacred oils,
The finest temple incense
        that thrills the nostrils of each god;
Let me relate all that has happened to me
        as well as what I know at first hand of your power
So they may properly praise God for your existence
        before the courts and councils of the Land;
Let me kill bulls to burn as offerings to you
        and wring the necks of birds;
Let me have them bring the fleet
        heaped with the fabled wealth of Egypt—
As one does for any god much loved by men
        who lives in a far country dimly known."

He laughed at me for what I told him—
        wrongly, to his way of thinking—
                saying:
"Yours is no great supply of myrrh
        though it happens you have incense;
Why, I myself rule Punt,
        the myrrh from there is mine.
And that poor sacred oil you spoke of bringing—
        it is the main thing on this island!
Now, you in due time will remove from here
        nevermore to see my island
                which shall turn to trackless sea."

At last the ship arrived
        just as he had foretold.
I climbed a lofty tree
        and recognized the sailors in the ship
And went running to report it,
        but he already knew.

Then he said to me,
        "Fare well, fare well, my little man, off to your home
                to see your children.
Make my name a proverb in your city;
        my reputation rests with you."
I placed myself upon the ground,
        my arms raised gratefully to him.

Then he collected me a cargo
        of myrrh, the sacred oil, perfumes, spices,
Tishepes-spices, kohl, Punt perfume, giraffe tails,
        great lumps of incense, elephant tusks,
Hounds, long- and short-tailed monkeys, and every helpful thing;
        and I loaded all of it onto the ship.
I placed myself upon the ground again
        giving praise to God for him.

Then he said to me,
        "You shall reach your native land in two months time
To fill your arms with children
        and grow young again at home until you die."
Then I descended to the shore near where the ship was.
        I hailed the crew
And offered thanks beside the sea to the Lord of the Isle;
        and those on board did likewise.

It was a voyage that we then made northwards
        toward the royal city of the King;
And we arrived home after two months,
        just as he had said.
Then I entered to my Sovereign
        and presented him these gifts
                which I had fetched him from the island.
He offered thanks to God for my existence
        before the courts and councils of the Land;
And I was made a royal Follower
        and given two hundred servants.
Just look at me, once I touched land!
        and after seeing all that I had seen!

Now, let what I have told sink in, my leader—
        you know, things people say can help you!"

Then he replied,
        "Don't try to play the expert, friend.
Does one give water to a sacrificial bird
        the morning of its execution day?"

Two Spells

S PELLS WERE composed and recited in order to bring about desired effects by supernatural means, often with the aid of the gods. The first here translated is a love spell used by a male to secure the affections of his beloved. It appears on an ostracon dating to the Ramesside period of the New Kingdom (ca. 1300–1100 B.C.). The second poem is from the much earlier Coffin Texts of the First Intermediate Period and the Middle Kingdom (ca. the twenty-second to nineteenth centuries B.C.). Here the reciter seeks to obtain the breath of life from the Four Winds in order to function in the otherworld and to see the face of God. There is heavy emphasis on knowing the secret names of the personages; for thereby one gains power over them.

Spell for Causing the Beloved to Follow After

Hear me, O Re, Falcon of Twin Horizons,
                              father of gods!
Hear me, you seven Hathors
                    who weave fate with a scarlet thread!
O Hear, all you gods of heaven and earth!—

                    Grant
That this girl, true child of her mother,
                         pursue me with undying passion,
Follow close on my heels
                    like a cow seeking pasture,
                         like a nursemaid minding her charge,
                              like a guardian after his herd!

For if you will not cause her to love me,
    I must surely abandon the day
        consumed to dust in the fire of my burning.

Spell for Power from the Four Winds of Heaven

These winds have been offered me by the Maidens:
The North Wind is she who caresses sea-washed islands,
    spreads wide her welcoming arms to the ends of earth,
Grows quiet at night
    to further her lover's designs each new day.
She is the breath of life, the North Wind,
    offered to me
        and through her I live.

These winds have been offered me by the Maidens:
The East Wind is she who raises the lashes of seeing,
                                discloses dawn,
    makes glittering way for the footstep of God
        when he strides over eastern horizon.
    Oh, let Re hold fast to my arm,
    Place me there in his field,
                    at peace amid rushes,
    There leave me eating and drinking forever,
        blessed by Osiris and Seth.
She is the breath of life, the East Wind,
    offered to me
        and through her I live.

These winds have been offered me by the Maidens:
This is the West Wind, brother to Ha,
                fiery lord of the Libyan desert,
    offspring and image of Iaaw,

bird god of ancestral Lapwings,
Alive since the day of the One People
(before ever the share became Two),
companion still to the Land one once more.
He is the breath of life, the West Wind
offered to me
and through him I live.

These winds have been offered me by the Maidens:
This is the South Wind, African,
who flows from the ancient Source,
god bringing Egypt water
that life be sturdy and prosper.
He is the breath of life, the South Wind,
offered to me
and through him I live.

Be praised, O you four Winds of heaven,
unseen spirits of sky,
I call you each by your Name,
by the unspeakable Name They gave you;
And I know your manner of birth,
once your Name appeared in the world
Back before man was conceived,
before even gods came to be,
Before ever birds had been snared,
before the taming of cattle,
Before the Wailer's jaws were tied shut,
daughter of Dawnstar,
before ever Mind mastered Trouble—
possessor of heaven and earth.

I sought these Names from the Lord of Powers,
and he it is gave them to me.

"Come, come along, to ferry the skyways together!
    I grant you to view the skyship,
                                embark,
        sail waves of the starry sea."

"No, no! It is I myself who fashioned a vessel
    to cross to the precinct of God;
And there, I shall launch the thousand-foot ship
    and sail to the Staircase of Fire!"

Confronting the Sun, before the bright face of God,
    may he sail to the Staircase of Fire!

The Testament of Amenemhat, King of Egypt

THIS INSTRUCTION of a royal father to his son dates to the reigns of Amenemhat I and Senusert I of Dynasty XII in the first half of the twentieth century B.C. The old king has been slain in a palace coup and returns as a ghost (much like Hamlet's father) to explain to his royal son and followers just what had happened in their absence. In the course of his appearance he gives some realistic and sometimes bitter advice to his son, at the same time offering an apologia for his life. The vocabulary and poetry of this piece are especially vivid; and Amenemhat's affection for his son, in particular, well survives the forty centuries since the poem was composed.

Here begins the testament
    made by the Majesty of Egypt, King Sehetep-ib-re,
Son of the Sun, Amenemhat,
    true of voice,
That which he uttered as an accurate accounting
    to his royal son, the Lord of All,
        and which he uttered risen as a god:

Hear what I have to say
    that you be sovereign of the Land indeed,
And rule the riverbanks of all the world,
    and reap abundance of good fortune.

Be on your guard with underlings who never prove,
        who do not true their hearts with their intentions;
            do not be near them when you walk alone.
Fill not your heart with brothers, do not know a friend,
        nurture no intimates—there is no good in these things.

At rest, trust in your watching heart alone;
>for none are there to help a man
>>when the day of trouble dawns.

I gave to the poor and raised the humble,
>advanced the man from nowhere like the man of means;
But it was he who ate my food who mustered troops,
>the one I circled with my arms hatched plots therein,
Those clothed with my fine linen thought me dressed in weeds,
>and those perfumed with myrrh spilled out my water.

Still-living likenesses of me, my heirs among mankind,
>make me such outcry as the world has not yet heard,
>>such fighting as has never yet been seen!
Yet do not take to battle not knowing yesterday;
>good never comes to one without the truth:

It was after dinner, night was come,
>and I had sought an hour of relaxation;
I rested on my bed, I drowsed,
>my mind began to follow after sleep—
And then there seemed a brandishing of swords, an asking for me,
>and I was furtive like a snake among the tombs.

I woke to fighting, once my mind was back,
>and found it an assault upon the guard.
If I had quickly taken weapons in my hand,
>I would have sent the reptiles packing to their holes;
But there is no man brave at night, none who can fight alone,
>nor can good fortune fall, wanting a defender.

And see what happened! Foul murder, while I was without you,
>before the courtiers could hear what I bequeathed you.
Now I shall never mount the throne beside you,
>>furthering your counsel.
>I was not steeled for this! I did not think it!

Nor could my heart conceive default by trusted servants.
Can it be that women marshal armies?
And does one nurture vipers in the home?
Or loose the torrent that destroys the fields
when one can only hurt the poor who work them?

Harm never reared behind me since my birth,
nor was my twin in bravery ever born!
I traveled the far South, turned back to Delta marshes,
stood on the edges of the world and saw its contours,
Attained the outer limits of this mighty Egypt
with my strong arm and in my many incarnations.

It was I who brought forth grain, the grain god loved me,
the Nile adored me from his every source;
One did not hunger during my years, did not thirst;
they sat content with all my deeds,
remembering me fondly;
and I set each thing firmly in its place.
I bated lions, captured crocodiles;
I conquered Nubians and brought back Medjai,
and I made Asiatics crawl like dogs.

I reared myself a dwelling chased with gold:
its ceilings lapis lazuli, its walls of silver,
Its flooring sycamore, its doors of copper,
the doorbolts were of bronze—
Made for eternity, made ready for all time;
and now I am sole Lord, world without end.

Many of the royal Family live here still—
the wise affirm my words, the ignorant demur
because they did not understand without your presence.
Senusert, royal Son, my feet are leaving;
yet would my heart draw near, my eyes still gaze upon you.

The Family now enjoy peace and good fortune,
    and those among the Sunfolk give you praise.

All that I did at first I interwove at last for you—
    I brought to harbor what was in my heart:
The gods are worshipped, White Crown worn
                              by offspring of the god,
    and all is well that I began for you.

I have descended to the barque of Re,
    rise to the kingship that has been since time began;
And do not act in my stead faithlessly,
    but raise the godly Images, furnish your final home,
And shield the wisdom of an upright heart
    because you always loved to have it by your side.

Hymn to Osiris

N
O GOD WAS more fundamental to the consciousness of the ancient Egyptians than Osiris, god of resurrection and king of the afterworld. Re and Amun were equally significant; but their roles were different as gods of creation or the cosmos, either in form visible (Re, the sun) or invisible (Amun, the "hidden"). The story of Osiris is that of a benevolent king murdered through envy of his goodness, who died and rose again, restored to life by his sister-wife, the great goddess Isis, and posthumously the father of a son, Horus, who avenged the evil done to his father by appeal to the tribunal of the Nine Great Gods of the universe. Justice and the balance of things were restored by awarding Horus his rightful inheritance, the land of Egypt. The example of Osiris assured the Egyptian of resurrection into a happy eternal life; and in later dynasties each person thought of himself or herself as "an Osiris" who would be born again forever. The text derives from the stela of one Amenmose, who lived during Dynasty XVIII (1551–1305 B.C.).

I

Turn your face gentle upon us, Osiris!

Lord of the life eternal, king of the gods,
Unnumbered the names of his protean nature,
     holy his manifold visible forms,
         hidden his rites in the temples.
First in Busiris is he, that noble spirit,
     abundant his wealth in Letopolis,
Hailed in the ancestral home of Andjeti,
     finely provided in Heliopolis;
God who remembers still
     down in the halls where men must speak true,
Heart of the inexpressible mystery,

lord of regions under the earth,
Worshipped in white-walled Memphis, power that raises the sun,
    whose earthly form rests in Heracleopolis;
Long echo his chants in the Pomegranate nome
    where the sacred tree sprang, a perch for his soul;
Who dwells in the high Hermopolitan temple,
    most awful god in Hypselis,
Lord of forever, first in Abydos,
    yet far off his throne in the red land of death.

His tale endures in the mouths of men:
    god of the elder time,
Belonging to all mankind—
    he gave earth food,
Finest of the Great Nine,
    most fruitful among the divinities.

II

It was for him chaos poured forth its waters
    and the north wind drove upstream;
Sky would make breeze for his nostrils
    that thereby his heart might find peace;
For his sake green things grew, and the
    good earth would bring forth its riches.
Sky and its stars obeyed him,
    for him the great gates of heaven stood open;
Praise of him thundered down southern skies,
    he was adored under northern heavens;
The circling, unfaltering stars
    wheeled near his watchful eye,
And the weary ones, who sink below seeing—
    with them was his very dwelling.

III

And he went forth in peace
    bearing the mace of Earth, his father,

and the Nine Great Gods gave worship;
Those in the underdark kissed ground,
    grateful dead in the desert bowed,
Gone generations joyed when they saw him,
    those seated Beyond stood in awe,
And the Two Lands united worshipped him,
    welcomed the advent of majesty.
Lordly leader, first of the eminent,
    whose kingdom endures to eternity—
His rule made kingship distinguished;
    power for good of the godhead,
Gracious and kind,
    whom to see is to love.
He made the nations revere him, that mankind might
    lift up his name before all they offered him;
Rememberer of whatever was, whether in heaven or earth,
    his mind entire in the land of forgetting;
Unending the shouts and the dancing at festival—
    rites for him of rejoicing
        done by Two Lands with one will.

IV

First-ranked of his brothers, the gods,
    noblest of the Great Nine,
He made order the length of the Riverbank,
    set a son at last on his throne,
Pride of his father, Geb,
    beloved of Nut, his mother.
With strength of the leopard he threw down the rebel,
    with powerful arm slew his opponent,
        put fear on his fallen enemy,
Reached the far borders of evil, uprooted,
    unflinching, set foot on his foe.
He inherited earth from his father,
    earned the Two Lands as their king.

V

For when Geb saw how perfect he was, he gave over his throne,
      gave him to guide the world to good fortune;
And this earth he delivered into his care—
      its waters, its air, its pastures and forage,
All of its walking creatures,
      what leaps into flight or flutters down,
Its creepers and crawlers,
      and the wild desert things—
All given as his to the son of Sky;
      and the Two Lands approved the succession.

V I

And he rose splendid, ascended the seat of his father in glory,
      like Re when he shines from horizon;
He put dawn on the blank face of darkness,
      igniting the sun with his double plume;
And he flooded the Two Lands with well-being
      like the sundisk rising at day.
His gleaming crown pierced heaven,
      became a brother to stars.
And he lived and ruled, a pattern for deity—
      good king governing well—
Praised and admired by greatest gods
      while lesser divinities loved.

V I I

His sister served as shield and defender,
      beat off the enemies,
Ended unspeakable mischief by power of her spell,
      golden-tongued goddess
          (her voice shall not fail),
Skilled to command,
      beneficent Isis,
          who rescued her brother.

Who searched for him
　　　and would not surrender to weariness,
Wandered this earth bent with anguish,
　　　restless until she had found him.
And she made him shade with her feathers,
　　　brought air by fanning her wings,
Performed the rites of his resurrection,
　　　moored, married, made breathe her brother,
Put life in the slackened limbs
　　　of the good god whose heart had grown weary.
And she took to herself his seed, grew big with the heritor,
　　　suckled and taught the child apart
　　　　　(his refuge not to be known),
Presented him, with his arm grown hardy,
　　　at Court in the broad hall of Geb.

VIII

And the Nine Great Gods were glad:
　　　"Welcome, Horus, son of Osiris!
Whose heart shall endure, whose cry shall find justice,
　　　son of Isis and heir of Osiris!"
Assembled for him the Tribunal of Truth—
　　　Nine Gods and the Lord of the Universe—
Oh, the Lords of Truth, they gathered within there,
　　　the Untempted by Evil took seats in Geb's hall
To offer the legacy to its just owner
　　　and the kingship to whom it belonged.
And they found it was Horus, his voice spoke true:
　　　and they gave him the realm of his father.

IX

And he went forth bearing the mace of Geb;
　　　and he took the scepter of the Two Banks;
　　　　　and the crown stood firm on his head.

Allotted to him was earth, to be his possession,
      heaven and earth alike put under his care;
Entrusted to him mankind—
      nobles, and commons, and sunfolk;
And the dear land of Egypt,
      the islands set in the northern sea,
Whatever the sun's disk circles—
      all these were given his governing—
And the good north wind, and the River, the flood,
      the plants men eat, and all that grows green.
And Nepri, Lord of the risen grain, he helped him
      to nurture fruits of the vital earth
So that Horus might bring on abundance,
      give it as gift to the nations.
And all mankind grew happy, hearts warmed,
      thoughts danced, and each face saw joy.

X

And they all gave thanks for his kindness:
      "How sweet is the love of him, say we;
His charm, it has ravished the heart.
      Great is the love for him in every person!"

And they offered this song for the son of Isis:

"His antagonist is down for his wrongdoing,
      since evil injures the mischiefmaker;
He who was hot to cause trouble,
      his deed recoils upon him
As Horus, son of Isis,
      who for him rescued his father:
            Hallowed be, and exalted, his name!
Majesty, it has taken its throne,
      Egypt's grandeur is sure under law;
The highroad is safe, bypaths lie beckoning—
      how ordered the banks of the River!

Wrongdoing, it weakens,
     injustice shall all pass away!
Earth lives in peace under its lord,
     Ma'at, Lady Truth, stands firm for her master,
       Man turns his back upon evil."

X I

"Hale be your heart, Osiris,
     you who were truly good,
       for the son of Isis has taken the crown!
Adjudged to him is his father's kingdom
     down in the broad hall of Geb.
Re it was uttered this; Thoth wrote it down;
     and the Grand Tribunal concurred.
Osiris, your father decreed in your favor!

     All he said has been faithfully done."

Hymn to the Nile

UNLIKE THE other major gods of Egypt, Hapy, the god of the Nile River, did not have a special city or cult center for worship; and no temples were raised in his honor. As the deified spirit or energy exhibited in the annual inundation, he brought the fertility and abundance without which the civilization of Egypt could not have existed. As its inhabitants well knew, Egypt was "the gift of the Nile"; and several hymns were composed in Hapy's honor. This piece is thought to derive from the Middle Kingdom and was possibly written by Khety in Dynasty XII (not the King Khety of *The Instruction for Merikare*). Ancient scribes of the New Kingdom called this Khety the best of all Egyptian writers.

I

May your countenance shine on us, Hapy, god of the moving River,
    who comes forth from earth
        returning to save the Black Land.
His features are hidden, dark in the daylight,
    yet the faithful find him fit subject for song.
He waters the landscape the Sun god has formed,
    giving life to every small creature,
Assuaging even the thirsty hills, far from the water's edge—
    for his is the rain, as it falls from heaven;
Loved by the waiting Earth, he nurtures the newborn Grain,
    and crafts of the Fashioner flourish in Egypt.

I I

Lord of the fish, he sends wildfowl flying south,
    and no bird falls prey to the stormwind;
He fathers the barley, brings emmer to be,
    fills the gods' temples with odor of festival.

But let him be backward, then breathing falters,
     all faces grow fierce with privation;
Should the gods' primal shrines lie dry in the dust,
     men by the millions were lost to mankind.

III

Absent, he unleashes greed to ravage the face of the land—
     famous and small wander homeless on highways;
And he baffles mankind as to when he draws near,
     for wayward he is, since the day Khnum made him.
Yet when sparkling he rises, the land stands rejoicing,
     every belly is filled with elation,
Bones of the creatures are shaken by laughter,
     teeth gleam, bared by welcoming smiles.

IV

Food bringer, rich with provisions,
     himself the author of all his good things,
Awe-striking master, yet sweet the aromas rising about him,
     and, how he satisfies when he returns!—
Transforming the dust to pastures for cattle,
     bringing forth for each god his sacrifice.
He dwells in the underworld, yet heaven and earth
                     are his to command,
     and the Two Lands he takes for his own,
Filling the storerooms, heaping the grainsheds,
     giving his gifts to the poor.

V

He causes each kind of good wood to grow tall,
     and no one in Egypt lacks timber,
Making the ship move through force of his flow,
     so it will not settle like stone.
Yet bluffs are borne off by his fierce upsurging,
     while he himself is not seen;

He goes to his work, and will not be governed
      though they chant out the secret spells;
Man cannot know the place where he is,
      nor his grotto be spied in the writings.

V I

Flood undercuts village rises, dykes will not hold,
      sight wanders, confused, with no landmarks to guide it.
Yet hordes of the young join his following,
      they hail him as sovereign lord,
For he anchors the earthly rhythms, returning in his due season,
      reclaiming the Twin Lands of Sedge and Papyri:
Each eye shines with moisture by means of him,
      all are rich through his flooding kindness.

V I I

Poised for his entrance, he rushes forth gladly,
      and each stranded heart floats on joy.
It was he begot Sobek, son of the Lady of Waters
      (how blessed indeed the Great Nine he fathered!)—
He foams across fields, sails over his marshland,
      impregnating earth for all men;
Yet he makes one strong while stripping another,
      nor can judgment be rendered against him;
He serves his own altars, refuses the time-honored rituals,
      endows for himself no gleaming stone temple.

V I I I

He illumines those who go forth in darkness—
      lighting their way with tallow of cattle;
The loom of events, it is his Power weaving,
      and no nome of the living lacks him.
He has clothed men with flax since first it was sown,
      affording Hedj-hetep help with his tasks,
Brewing resins and oils for the god of orchards

so Ptah will have glues to fasten things tight;
He readies works of the field for Khepri to rise upon—
     there are workers themselves only because of him;
All writing belongs to the Word of God,
     and he it was supplied the papyri.

IX

He descends to the netherworld, rises again,
     Revealer, returning with news of the Mysteries;
But if listless he lies, his subjects are few—
     he kills them by letting the green world wither.
Then no better than women see Thebans,
     each man in despair destroying his gear:
No raw goods for finishing handwork,
     no cloth for the weaving of clothes,
No decking out offspring of rich men,
     no shadowing beautiful eyes,
For lack of him, the trees all in ruins—
     no perfumes to linger on anyone.

X

He plants a sense of due Order deep in the hearts of mankind,
     lest men forswear the helpless among them;
In perfect accord he joins with the Great Green Sea
     nor seeks to control the sweep of its waters;
He offers each god due praise and worship
     while letting no bird fall to his desert.
There is no grasping of his hand after gold—
     for no man slakes thirst drinking money,
One cannot eat precious stone and be nourished—
     food first, let prosperity follow.

XI

Songs to the harp are begun for him,
     chanters and singers clap hands,
Troops of the young shout for joy to him,

the irrepressible crowd is arrayed:
For he comes! bringing riches, burnishing bright the dull land,
    renewing the color and flesh of mankind,
Fostering dreams of women with child,
    wanting hosts of the whole world of creatures.

XII

When godlike he shines amid hungry townsmen,
    by his fruits of the field are they satisfied.
He provides for the lotus its new show of blossoms,
    and all that feeds green things overflows earth;
The pastures are crowded with children—
    they have forgotten how hungry they were;
Good streams through the streets and squares,
    the length of the land frisks and flowers.

XIII

Hapy rides high, and thanksgiving is offered him:
    for him longhorned cattle are slaughtered,
For him the festival meal prepared,
    fowl are made fat for him,
Lions trapped out on the desert,
    debts of kindness repaid him;
And to each god they make offering
    just as is done for Hapy:
Incense, birds, beasts big and small—all are given;
    and down in his cave Hapy stirs, irresistible.
Yet not in the underworld shall his name be known,
    nor can the very gods reveal it.

XIV

All men honor the Nine Great Gods,
    but They stand in awe of that deity
Who aids his son, divine Lord of All,
    in greening the banks of the Nile.
O hidden god, be it well with you! may you flourish, and return!

Hapy, river-spirit, may you flourish and return!
Come back to Egypt, bringing your benediction of peace,
 greening the banks of the Nile;
Save mankind and the creatures, make life likely,
 through the gift of all this your countryside!
 O hidden god, be it well with you! may you flourish, and return!
 Hapy, Lord of Egypt, may you flourish and return!

The Maxims of Ptahhotep

T HIS INSTRUCTION was presumably composed during Dynasty V of the Old Kingdom since Ptahhotep served as vizier under King Izezi (ca. 2380-2340 B.C.). *The Maxims* are one of the most celebrated of such collections of wisdom, which comprise the experience garnered by a father, usually from a successful public career, and handed down to a son. Such texts constituted the "philosophy" of all ancient Near Eastern cultures. The preeminence of such wisdom texts in the Egyptian tradition is seen in the fact that only they tend to have authors' names attached to them, the remainder of the literature now being virtually anonymous. Such authors were regarded as the sages of the civilization. *The Maxims* are exemplified here by the author's opening comments on the travails of old age and by the first maxim.

Prologue

The Teaching of the Mayor of the Royal City and Vizier, Ptahhotep, under the Majesty of the King of Upper and Lower Egypt, Izezi, who lives for ever and ever. The Mayor of the Royal City and Vizier, Ptahhotep, says:

"My sovereign Lord,
Old age has come, the years weigh heavily,
    misery my lot, and infant helplessness returns.
Repose for such a one is sleeplessness each day;
    the eyes are dim, the ears benumbed,
Strength ebbs from the faltering heart,
    the mouth is still and cannot speak,
The mind is gone and cannot picture yesterday,
    bones ache from head to toe,

The nose is clogged and cannot breathe the air,
        it makes no difference if you stand or sit.
Good turns to ill,
        experience has passed you by:
What old age does to all mankind
        is heartbreak every way.

May you appoint your servant one to lean on in old age;
        then shall I pass to him words of the judges,
The wisdom of our forebears,
        those in the past who listened to the gods.
Then shall the like be done for you
        that the troubles of the people be defeated
            and the Two Banks work for you."

        Then the Majesty of this god said:
"Yes, teach him according to the speech of old;
        then he shall be a pattern for offspring of the great,
So that understanding shall sink in by means of him,
        each heart a witness to what he has said.

"No one is born wise."

Maxim 1

Do not be arrogant because of your knowledge;
    approach the unlettered as well as the wise.
The summit of artistry cannot be reached,
    nor does craftsman ever attain pure mastery.
More hidden than gems is chiseled expression
    yet found among slave girls grinding the grain.

Menna's Lament,
or
Letter to a Wayward Son

THIS POEM APPEARS on a magnificent ostracon now in Chicago. Menna, the father, and his son, Pay-iry, are historical personages of Ramesside times (ca. 1300–1100 B.C.) who lived in the village of Deir el-Medineh on the east bank of ancient Thebes. The villagers were the ones who constructed and decorated the rock-cut tombs of the New Kingdom pharaohs in the Valley of the Kings. The ostracon derives ultimately from that village and its school for young scribes; and the letter is a literary rendering of a sad event that may actually have taken place. Pay-iry, instead of remaining at home and taking up his father's craft, runs off to sea. The bereft father writes in an attempt to persuade him to return.

The artist Menna
speaks to his son and apprentice,
the scribe Pay-iry:

High winds foretell for you the coming of the storm,
    my able seaman, lost for the final mooring.

I had set good advice of every sort
    before you—but you never listened.
I would point out each path
    which hid the danger in the underbrush,
Saying, "Should you go without your sandals,
    one little thorn will end your caravan."
I satisfied your needs in everything
    that normal men desire;

56

Nor would I let you cry "If only!" in the night,
        tossing and turning as you lay in bed.

Yet you are like the swallow in her flight
        wide wandering with her fledgling brood;
And when you reach the Delta in your great migration,
        you run with foreign Asiatic birds—
You have fed on your own vitals
        and neither heart nor sense is left within you!

I am so troubled I would range the sea
        might I report that I had rescued you;
Yet would you come to enter your own village
        bringing but water for your monument.

I said in my heart, "He does not care for words,
        for any I have spoken up 'til now."

But I must say again what I have said before:

Get you from the ramparts of the wicked.
        Fortify yourself with maxims of the wise,
In speech, in name, in deed;
        and your ship of fools may still do likewise.
Then, should it founder far out in the East,
        men would address you with the honor due a lion
            although you stood alone.

As for the son who should obey his father,
        that text holds good for all eternity, they say.
But then you did not pause for any admonition
        with which I warned and warned you long ago.

Should you capsize when you take ship defying me—
        should you drift downward to a watery grave—

Should you stride wide upon the waves to flee the deep—
        still were you lost through your own piloting!

And who shall speak the word to my small boat,
        "Go to him swiftly over the white-capped waves"?
I see you sinking in the chambers of the sea,
        and my arm does not know how to save you!
All I can bring you is a slender straw
        thrown in the wide path of the drowning man. . . .
                There is not any way at all.

You make yourself like one who says
        that you would kill to have my donkeys,
                choking the very protests in my mouth!
You clip the wings of him who eyes your goods,
        yet are you dull and dawdling in my presence;
Your goods themselves aggrandize only senseless people
        because you chose to act without me.

You should take care to weigh my words,
        and you might find my teaching useful;
Give ear to hear instruction
        so as to build on long experience.
Should I allow you to ignore it altogether,
        you will shoot up a useless weed;
There is no climbing to the height for such a one
        though he provide you with an ample household.

Oh, that a son of mine should be found out
        letting this hell-bent course continue!
You are like someone on a team of bolting horses,
        yet should your heart beat easy in the reins with mine!

My son, preserve and hold in trust this letter.
        Someday, it might bring you good.

Lament to Amun

T HIS IS A prayer found on a New Kingdom papyrus dating to approximately 1200 B.C. The writer describes a world gone wrong and asks God to help him escape it.

"Come to me, Father Amun,
      protect me in this bitter year of confrontation.
God shines in the sun, yet he will not shine;
      winter crowds hard upon summer.
Months happen backwards;
      disheveled hours lurch drunken by.
Those cut down in high places cry out to you, Amun;
      the beaten in alleyways seek you;
And the new generation at the breasts of its nurses
      wails, 'Give us our *Lebensraum*, Father!'
God find in his heart to return, bringing peace,
      bringing air, the clean breeze before him.
Or let him grow me the wings of protection
      to soar like his skyship high beyond earth."

These words came on the poisoned air,
Spoken by herdsmen in fields and marshes,
      by those who beat clothes on the banks of the River,
By district police deserting their precincts,
      by horned beasts on our burning deserts.

Longing for Memphis

T HE SPEAKER OF this poem is an apprentice scribe weary of his schoolwork and daydreaming of the big city. He prays to Ptah, god of Memphis, to help him concentrate on his lesson. The text is from a student's "miscellany" of New Kingdom date.

Farewell, my thoughts!   Absconded,
  they race toward a place they know well,
Upriver bound to see Memphis, House of Lord Ptah.
  (And I wish I were with them!)

But I idle here absentminded, wanting my thoughts back
  to whisper me news of the City.
No task at all now prospers by this hand—
  heart, torn from its perch, just not in it.

  (Come to me, Ptah! Carry me captive to Memphis,
   let me gaze all around . . . and fly free!)

I would spend my workday wakeful and dutiful,
  but the will drowses, heart
Veers away, will not stay in my body;
  all other parts of me sickened to ennui—
The eye heavy with staring and studying;
  ear, it will not be filled with good counsel;
Voice cracks, and words of the recitation
         tumble and slur.

O Lord of the City friendly to young scribes,
  be at peace with me!
    Grant me to rise above this day's infirmities!

For a Portrait of the Queen in Luxor Temple

T HIS POEM, actually a love song, was carved into the wall of the temple at Luxor around the middle of the thirteenth century B.C. and commemorates Nefertari, great royal wife of King Ramesses II, the pharaoh who ruled Egypt for most of that century. There is a charming contrast between the public situation of the poem and its loving description of the queen.

This was a princess.
Of the line royal, lady most praiseworthy
and a woman of charm, sweet for love,
Yet Mistress ruling two countries,
the Twin Lands of Sedge and Papyri.

See her, her hands here shaking the sistra
to bring pleasure to God, her father Amun.
How lovely she moves,
her hair bound with fillets,
Songstress with perfect features,
a beauty in double-plumed headdress,
And first among harîm women
to Horus, Lord of the Palace.

Pleasure there is in her lips' motions,
all that she says, it is done for her gladly,
Her heart is all kindness, her words
gentle to those upon earth.
One lives just to hear her voice.

On this wall, by this door, she stands singing,
Great Royal Wife of the Sovereign
    (and a girl King Ramesses loved),
Consort to Power and Majesty,
    she is Queen of the Realm, Nefertari.

The Leiden Hymns

THIS CYCLE OF poems appears on a papyrus dated to the fifty-second regnal year of Ramesses II, circa 1238 B.C. The hymns, thus, are from this period or somewhat earlier. Their author used the strange device of numbering the hymns consecutively by units from one to ten, then by tens up to one hundred, and finally by hundreds up to eight hundred, when the papyrus breaks off. There were probably about twenty-eight hymns in the entire composition, though the first five and the last two are now missing. In *The Leiden Hymns* we see a culmination of ancient Egyptian theology as it developed the conception of one preeminent God, the creator, all-powerful, all-encompassing, god of all lands and peoples, and one who can appear in a multitude of forms or incarnations, including those of the other Egyptian gods. God is called "Amun" or "Amun-Re"; but as we read the poems, we realize that the poet-theologian who composed these pieces is expressing the mystery of the one God. He moves in unfathomable ways and takes many forms to human comprehension—as the various poems demonstrate; but though he is hidden from human sight, he is indeed the ultimate godhead, God alone.

Hymn 9

The Nine Great Gods are come from the waters,
      gathered to worship the dayspring of Majesty,
Lord of Lords, who made himself God out of nothing,
      Lord of all deities, he is the Lord.

And those who must sleep and awaken, he shines for them too
      to brighten their faces in visible form:
His eyes glow kindly, his ears are listening,
      and each naked creature is clothed in his light.

Sky turns to gold, turquoise the primeval waters,
 the Southland is lapis lazuli blue
   as he rises shining upon them;
Gods of the old days marvel, their temples lie open,
 even late man peeps out and wonders.

Trees sway, nod and bow before him,
 look to the one source, arms wide with blossoms;
The scaly ones flash in the water,
 bold from their hidden crannies for love of him;
Small beasts are gay in his sight,
 birds flutter and run with stretched wings.

The creatures most truly know him
  at this hour of his rising beauty—
 life itself is to see him each day;
They lie in his hand, signed in his own hieroglyphic,
 and no god but God breaks the seal of their love.

There are none who can live without him;
 he is indeed Great God,
  Power that moves all deity.

Hymn 10

The legend of Thebes exceeds any city.
    In the Beginning
        hers were the waters and dry land;
Then sands came to mark off fields,
    to form her foundations on that high hill
        back when the world came to be;
And then there were faces of men
    to establish the cities, each with its calling;
And all have names after their natures
    by order of Thebes, God's Eye over Egypt.

The Majesty of Thebes came down as his salvation
    to draw the world, through her, to the Spirit of God,
Pleased to dwell by the waters of Asheru
    in the likeness of Sakhmet, Mistress of Egypt.
How strong she is! without contender,
    she honors her name as Queen of the Cities.
Sharp-sighted, keen as God's protector,
    Right Eye of Re,
        disciple facing her Lord,
Bright with the glory of God,
    wise upon her high throne,
    she is Most Holy of Places,
        a mecca the world cannot parallel.

Each city stirs into life at the breath of invisible God,
    burns to be great. Like Thebes:
        hers is the light of perfection.

Hymn 20

How splendid you ferry the skyways,
                Horus of Twin Horizons,
The needs of each new day
                firm in your timeless pattern,
Who fashion the years,
                weave months into order—
Days, nights, and the very hours
                move to the gait of your striding.

Refreshed by your diurnal shining, you quicken,
                bright above yesterday,
Making the zone of night sparkle
                although you belong to the light,
Sole one awake there
                —sleep is for mortals,
Who go to rest grateful:
                your eyes oversee.
And theirs by the millions you open
                when your face new-rises, beautiful;
Not a bypath escapes your affection
                during your season on earth.

Stepping swift over stars,
                riding the lightning flash,
You circle the earth in an instant,
                with a god's ease crossing heaven,
Treading dark paths of the underworld,
                yet, sun on each roadway,
You deign to walk daily with men.

                The faces of all are upturned to you,
As mankind and gods
                alike lift their morningsong:
"Lord of the daybreak,
                Welcome!"

Hymn 30

The harpoon is deep in Apophis, the Evil,
     he falls by the sword;
       and those who chose war are huddled for slaughter—
Death cuts the hearts of God's demon enemies,
     who groan as outlaws,
       apostate forever.
He has ordered the remnant sacrificed
     to cripple the power of the dark Adversary
       that God's own self be secure.

Unharmed is he in his midship chapel!
       the holy Light shines still!
He has ridden the waves unscathed
     and rebels are no more!
The sunship of infinite journeys
      still sails on course through the sky,
     her godly crew cheering,
      their hearts sweet with victory.
Down is the great Antagonist,
      bane of the Lord of Creation;
    no partisan of his is found
        either in heaven or earth!

Sky, Thebes, Heliopolis, Underworld—
     their peoples are proud of their conquering God,
For they see him strong in his sunrise epiphany
     robed in beauty and victory and power.
It is day!
    You have won, Amun-Re!
      Gone the dark children of Enmity,
       dead by the sword.

Hymn 40

God is a master craftsman;
> yet none can draw the lines of his Person.

Fair features first came into being
> in the hushed dark where he mused alone;

He forged his own figure there,
> hammered his likeness out of himself—

All powerful one (yet kindly,
> whose heart would lie open to men).

He mingled his heavenly god-seed
> with the inmost parts of his being,

Planting his image there
> in the unknown depths of his mystery.

He cared, and the sacred form
> took shape and contour, resplendent at birth!

God, skilled in the intricate ways of the craftsman,
> first fashioned Himself to perfection.

Hymn 70

God loosens the knot of suffering, tempers disease,
    physician who cures without ointments;
Clear-sighted, he unclouds the darkening vision,
    opens his hidden nature to men.
He will save whom he loves, though one walk in the underworld,
    free from the debt due fate
        as his heart, in wisdom, determines.

To Amun are eyes, and ears as well:
    face guarding every way for one he loves;
He hears the entreaty of any who cry to him,
    come in an instant to whoever summons him
        the distance no matter how far.
He can lengthen a life or wreak havoc within it,
    offer wealth beyond fated measure
        to that man blessed by his love.

He is a water spell: his Name hovers high—
    God's wings span the waters of Chaos;
No power at all to Death the Crocodile
    when one calls on God's name.

Winds of the deep contend, a withering storm veers nigh—
    yet eased a man's end by remembering him:
Spellbinding such speech at the moment of truth
    when man meets death face to face;
And breezes are soft for who calls upon God—
    he rescues the wind and wave weary.

For God is a god of mercy, mild in his dealing, fond;
    his children are all who bow to his lordship—
        upraised to the everpresence of God.
Sufficient is he above any

when housed in the human heart,
his Name alone
more potent than numberless deities.
He protects what is good in the world,
ready to take to himself any who falter behind;
there are none to oppose him.

Hymn 80

The Eight Great Gods were your first incarnation,
        to bring to perfection this cosmos.
              You were the alone;
Secret your image from even oldest divinities:
        you had hidden yourself as Amun from faces of gods.

You entered your form as Ta-tenen, and earth rose from chaos
        bearing the primal deities back in your elder time;
Erect grew your charms as Kamutef,
        life force, lusty son of his mother;
You withdrew to the midst of heaven, and distance was born,
        endured in the sun, forming time,
Returned as the father gods, and they begat sons,
        beginning the generations, creating
           a heritage fit for your progeny.

You began the unfolding of cosmos,
                before was no being, no void;
World without end was in you and from you,
                yours on that First Day.
      All other gods came after.

Hymn 90

The Nine Great Gods were drawn from your person,
        and in each you shadowed your features;
But it was you shone first
                when you fashioned the world long ago,
        O unseen God
                who hides himself from all others.

Ancient of ancients,
            elder even than they,
        earth god who fashioned himself into Ptah,
The very parts of whose body are primeval gods;
        who rose as the Sun amid chaos
To betoken rebirth
                    and the rhythms of resurrection;
Sowed the seed of the cosmos as Atum, the Old One,
        from whose godhead were moisture and air,
                Shu and Tefnut, the primordial couple.

He ascended in grandeur his throne
            as his heart had determined,
        by his power, alone, overruled all existence,
United himself and kingship forever
        to remain, to the end of days, sole Lord.

But in the Beginning, Light!
                Light was his first incarnation;
        and the incipient world lay hushed
                        waiting in awe of him;
And he cried the glad cry of the Great Cackler
        over the nomes of his new creation
                        while he was still alone.

He loosened speech:
            words flowed in the chambers of silence;

he opened each eye
                that it might behold and be gladdened.
Sounds of the voiceless world began with him:
        the victory shout of unparalleled God
                shattered silence and circled the world.
He nurtured to birth all things
        that he might offer them life,
        and he taught men to know the Way,
                the path they each must go.
Hearts come alive when they see him,
        for he is our Procreator, the Power
                who peopled the dark with his children.

Hymn 100

When Being began back in days of the genesis,
  it was Amun appeared first of all,
    unknown his mode of inflowing;
There was no god became before him,
  nor was other god with him there
    when he uttered himself into visible form;
There was no mother to him, that she might have
      born him his name,
  there was no father to father the one
    who first spoke the words "I Am!"
Who fashioned the seed of him all on his own,
  sacred first cause, whose birth lay in mystery,
    who crafted and carved his own beauty—
He is God the Creator, self-created, the Holy;
  all other gods came after;
    with himself he began the world.

Hymn 200

Dark be the changes, and dazzling the incarnations
        of God, god of wonders, of the two firmaments,
           god of the myriad visible forms.
All gods boast they share in his nature—
             but to heighten themselves,
      borrowing splendor on splendor
          from the terrible power of his godhead.

Re himself joins to shine in God's visible form,
        and God is that Craftsman praised in the city of Sun;
What is said of the earth god in truth pictures him;
       and when Amun emerged from out the ur-waters,
          it was God's image strode over them.
He flowed forth again as the Eight of Hermopolis,
       procreated the primal deities, was midwife to Re,
Perfected himself in Atum—one flesh together;
       and he alone, Lord of all things at creation.

His soul, they say, is that One above,
       and he is the one in halls of the underworld,
         foremost of those in the eastern dwelling;
His soul rests in heaven, his earthly form in the West,
       and his image in Thebes—for worship
         when he shows himself among men.

But, one alone is the hidden God,
       being behind these appearances,
   veiled even from gods,
       his nature cannot be known;
He is more distant far than heaven,
       deeper profound than the world below,
    not all gods in concert discern his true features.
No likeness of him is sketched on papyri,
    no eyewitness tellings to picture him.

God is loath to release his full glory,
      great beyond questioning, potent beyond all belief:
Dead on the instant in pain is that unfortunate god
      who utters—even in innocence—God's hidden Name.
No god draws forth godhead by this means;
      God is final, ineffable Spirit,
           past knowing his name and his mystery.

Hymn 300

God is three of all gods,
      Amun, Re, Ptah—these are preeminent:
Past knowing his nature as Amun, the hidden,
      he is Re in his features, in body is Ptah.
Their cities on earth endure to eternity,
      Thebes, Heliopolis, Memphis, forever;
Word from heaven is heard in the city of Sun,
      told in Ptah's temple to the Handsome of Face,
Who shapes it in signs for Thoth's books of wisdom;
      thus Amun's city records the gods' histories.
For God's judgment is rendered from Thebes:
      when decision emerges, it comes through the Ennead;
Since each move of his lips is most secret,
      gods carry out what he commands.
God's Word, it can kill or perpetuate,
      life or death for all men unfolds by means of it;
And he opens his countenance as Re, Ptah, or Amun,
      a trinity of unchanging forms.

Hymn 500

Defeated and doomed the rebels, down on their faces,
      none now dare to attack him;
Land freshens once more over erstwhile opponents,
      the dissatisfied cannot be found.

Rampant lion with knife-edged claws, in a swallow
      he drinks the power and blood of pretenders;
Bull, strong-backed and steady, whose hooves
      bear down on foe's neck while horns do their work;
Bird of prey who swoops to seize his assailant,
      talons keen to shred flesh and crack bone!

How he delights to do battle, secure in his puissant arm!
      Hills quake to his tread when the war-fit masters him,
Earth shakes as he bellows his war-cry,
      creation cowers in fear.
Oh, woe to any who challenge him,
      who taste the play of his twin-tipped weapon,
For he, our God, is skilled above any,
      Lord of the deadly horns.

Hymn 600

The mind of God is perfect knowing,
      his lips its flawless expression,
   all that exists is his spirit,
      by his tongue named into being;
He strides, and hollows under his feet become Nile-heads—
   Hapy wells from the hidden grotto into his footprints.
His soul is all space,
      his heart the life-giving moisture,
   he is falcon of twin horizons,
         sky god skimming heaven,
His right eye the day,
     while his left is the night,
   and he guides human seeing down every way.
His body is Nun, the swirling original waters;
       within it the Nile
   shaping, bringing to birth,
        fostering all creation;
His burning breath is the breeze,
     gift offered every nostril,
   from him too the destiny fallen to each;
His consort the fertile field,
     he shoots his seed into her,
   and new vegetation, and grain,
        grow strong as his children.
Fruitful One, Eldest,
     he fathered gods in those first days,
   whose faces turn to him
      daily and everywhere.
That countenance still shines on mankind and deities,
   and it mirrors the sum of the world.

The Harper's Song for Inherkhawy

ARPERS' SONGS are a strange survival from ancient Egypt. They seem to fly in the face of all religious tradition; for they express the *carpe diem* theme, "seize the day." As this poem clearly states, the end of life brings not a happy afterlife but the grave. Thus one must enjoy life while one can. The piece from Inherkhawy's tomb (Dynasty XX, ca. 1160 B.C.) is one of the finest expressions of this theme.

A Song

Sung by his Harpist for the Osiris,
Chief of the Crew in the Place of Truth,
Inherkhawy, who says:

I am this man, this worthy one,
  who lives redeemed by abundance of good
    tendered by God indeed.

I

All who come into being as flesh
        pass on, and have since God walked the earth;
            and young blood mounts to their places.

The busy fluttering souls and bright transfigured spirits
        who people the world below
            and those who shine in the stars with Orion,
They built their mansions, they built their tombs—
        and all men rest in the grave.

So set your home well in the sacred land
        that your good name last because of it;

Care for your works in the realm under God
    that your seat in the West be splendid.

The waters flow north, the wind blows south,
    and each man goes to his hour.

11

So, seize the day! hold holiday!
    Be unwearied, unceasing, alive,
        you and your own true love;
Let not your heart be troubled during your sojourn on earth,
    but seize the day as it passes!

Put incense and sweet oil upon you,
    garlanded flowers at your breast,
While the lady alive in your heart forever
    delights, as she sits beside you.

Grieve not your heart, whatever comes;
    let sweet music play before you;
Recall not the evil, loathsome to God,
    but have joy, joy, joy, and pleasure!

O upright man, man just and true,
    patient and kind, content with your lot,
        rejoicing, not speaking evil—
Let your heart be drunk on the gift of Day
    until that day comes when you anchor.

The Eloquent Peasant

T HIS TEXT DATING to the Middle Kingdom purports to depict events occurring during the reign of King Khety III Nebkaure of Dynasty X (ca. 2050 B.C.). A humble farmer and trader is robbed of his goods by a bureaucrat. He appeals his case to Rensi, the pharaoh's Lord High Steward; and because the eloquence of this humble man is so astounding, Rensi informs the king, who has the peasant detained until he has made nine such appeals. His family is secretly cared for during this period, and all his passionate oratory is carefully written down for the king. At the end, the peasant is rewarded and the petty bureaucrat punished. The theme of the peasant's nine speeches is *ma'at*, one of the most fundamental concepts of ancient Egyptian civilization, representing a union of our terms "truth," "justice," and "harmony." Here *ma'at* is translated as "justice." The peasant's speeches offer one of the earliest treatments ever of that concept.

The Peasant's Eighth Complaint

O Lord High Steward, my lord,
  we fall through curséd greed.
The greedy man, he comes to no good end—
  his seeming triumphs are but moral failure.
You too are greedy, it does not become you;
  you take, there is no benefit to you.

Oh, leave a man alone to seek his own true fortune!
  You have your own belongings in your house,
    your belly's full,
The barley springs so high it bends toward earth,
  its excess dropping to the ground to die.

The one who stops a thief aids the officials.
Do whatever shall oppose injustice.
The refuge of the hard-pressed man, it is those same officials.
Do whatever shall oppose deceit.

Fear of your high position hinders my appeal to you,
yet you cannot know my thoughts—
And so, your quiet man is back,
and he would make his grievance clear to you.
He should not fear the one to whom he puts his plea,
nor should his fellow find you absent from the streets.

Your fields lie all about the countryside,
your grain grows on your grounds,
Your foodstuffs fill the storehouse,
officials offer gifts to you—
And still you pillage!
Are you really such a robber?
Is it true whole gangs are dragged along with you
to confiscate those fields?

Do Justice for the Lord of Justice,
who is the wise perfection of his Justice.
Reed pen, papyrus, and palette of Thoth all dread to write injustice:
when good is truly good, that good is priceless—
But Justice is forever,
and down to the very grave it goes with him who does it.
His burial conceals that man within the ground,
yet his good name shall never perish from the earth;
The memory of him becomes a precious thing,
he is a standard written in the Word of God.
Is he a scales? It does not tilt.
Is he a balance beam? It does not dip awry.

Now, either I shall come, or surely someone else will come,
      and may you condescend an answer!
Do not detain your quiet man for questioning;
      do not attack one who did not injure you.
—You are not merciful, you do not care,
      and yet you cannot flee, you are not able to destroy;
And you certainly can never compensate me
                  for these splendid words
      which pour forth from the mouth of God himself!

Speak Justice! Do Justice!
      for it is powerful, it is far-reaching, it endures.
All that devotion to it shall discover
      leads on to honor and to veneration.
Does the balance tilt indeed?
      It is still the scalepan does the weighing.
There never can be excess of high standards,
      nor should a mean act reach the humblest habitation
      until we mingle with the earth.

The Tale of Sinuhe

T HIS TALE IS considered by many Egyptologists to be the finest piece of literature to survive from ancient Egypt. It is the story of a trusted courtier who ran away from an attempted coup, escaping into voluntary exile in Syria-Palestine, where he lives out most of his life alienated from his Egyptian roots. The tale shows him slowly working his way back to self-esteem and eminence. Toward the end of his life he is able to return to Egypt, where he is warmly welcomed by his king and the royal family whose servant he had been. Many of the fundamental values of ancient Egyptian civilization are expressed in this narrative. The now anonymous author conceived and executed the poem so splendidly that, on the basis of present evidence, he can rightly be called the Shakespeare of ancient Egypt. The tale is from Dynasty XII in the twentieth century B.C.

I

The man of ancient family, chief of his town,
   who bore the goddess' seal for Lower Egypt, Only Friend,
Senior overseer of waterways,
   viceroy for Asian lands,
Trusted adviser to the King, one he esteemed,
   the courtier Sinuhe.
      It is he who speaks:

I was a good and faithful servant of my Lord,
   attendant in the harîm
      of the Lady of noble blood, most highly favored,
King's Wife of Senusert
   seated as consort on the throne,
Daughter of Amenemhat

in the city of Qa-nefer,
Neferu,
gone long ago to bliss.

II

Regnal Year Thirty,
Third Month of the Inundation, Day Seven,
Day of Ascension: god mounts toward his last horizon,
King of the Sedge and the Bee, Sehetep-ib-re,
That he might soar to heaven, be one with the Sun,
flesh of the god mingling with God who made him.
The royal City is silent, the heart without consolation,
the Great Paired Gates are sealed;
Courtiers crouch, head bent on knee,
the people groan with grief.

Now see the situation: his Majesty passed on
and the army west in the Libyan desert,
His eldest son commanding,
the beneficent god, Crown Prince Senusert.
Sent to punish barbarian lands,
destroying all who would live among Libyans,
He was now returning with what he had taken—
doomed slaves from those desert tribes
and unnumbered cattle and livestock.

The council of royal advisers (the Palace Companions)
sent word to the western side
In order to let the king's son know
what had transpired in his father's chamber.
The envoys found him upon the march,
having come under cover of darkness.
Not a moment at all did he linger:
the Falcon, he flew with his followers
never letting his army know.

III

Somehow word reached the King's other sons
    (those with the prince on this expedition);
And Someone called one son aside in the dark
    while I—I was standing right there—
I heard his very voice while he spoke treason
    and I on the rising ground close by!
My heart then hung undone, fear paralyzed my arms,
    a shuddering shook my body.
But I made good retreat, and scurried off
    to find fit place to hide,
Cowering down within some bushes
    which screened the road from the runaway.

Then I continued on upstream,
    for I hardly meant to stop by the Residence:
I feared civil disorder—
    nor would I long outlive the late King.
I wandered the Maaty Canal, crossing it nearby Sycamore,
    and touched down on Sneferu's Island;
I spent the day resting there at the edge of the cultivation
    and set out bright the next dawn,
Startling a man standing square in my path
    who bowed low with respect, for he was afraid.
At last the dinner hour came on,
    and I had gained the landing near Cattleford.

I crossed the Nile in a rudderless boat
    blown on the breath of the west wind
And faded from sight east of the Quarry
    moving south of the Lady of Red Peak.
Then I offered the road to my feet, turning north,
    and skirted Walls-of-the-Ruler,
Built to ward off vile Asiatics
    and discourage bedouin wanderers.

I took to crouching down in the brush
      for fear of seeing the sentry
            who was up on the wall, on duty,
      and continued on and on through the night.

Day dawned, and I had reached Peten,
      alit on an isle of the Great Salt Sea.
Thirst fell, it drove me on;
      I was choking, my throat clogged with dust;
And I said to myself, "So this is the taste of death!"
      and steadied my heart for the end.

But then I heard the lowing of cattle
      and I saw . . . blest Asiatics!
The sheikh of that crew knew me
      (a man who often went down into Egypt),
So he gave me water to drink
      and afterward boiled me milk.
I returned with him to his bedouin people,
      and welcome it was, all they did for me!

Land gave me to land
      once I set out for Byblos, cutting the ties behind;
Then I turned east toward the Qedem hills,
      staying a year and a half in that region.

IV

Then Amunenshi fetched me away
      (he was ruler of Upper Retenu),
         saying,
"You would do well with me
      and you would hear the accents of Egypt."
He broached this knowing my reputation
      (he had already heard of my skill);
And native Egyptians vouched for me
      of those who were with him there.

Then he went on,
  "How in the world have you come this far?
   Has something occurred at the palace?"

And I replied,
  "Sehetep-ib-Re. Gone to his last horizon.
   One cannot know what happens after."
And I added (wide of the truth)
  that I had returned with the army from Libya:
"They told it to me, and my heart shook—
  my heart drove me out on the wide ways of flight.
I was not spat upon,
  nor did they lay charges against me.
I know not what brings me here to this land;
  it was a miracle of God—
As if a Delta man should find himself up-River
  or a bewildered marshman in the Nubian sand!"

At that he mused before me,
  "What will poor Egypt do
   lacking his help, that late and splendid god?
Respect for him pervades the world
  like fear of our Great Lady in a year of plague."

Thus he said, and thus I answered him,
  "Surely his son is risen to the palace,
   taking, himself, his father's heritage:

V

"For he is a god indeed, without an equal,
  no other came to be before him,
Lord of wisdom, wise in counsel,
  potent in commanding words;
Envoys come and go to do his bidding,
  and he it is subdues the foreign lands:

89

The father stays behind within the palace,
    the son reporting: what is ordered, it is done.

"He is a warrior too, of royal deeds,
    brave, with no likenesses among mankind.
He can be seen in majesty scattering alien hordes
    once he has joined the heat of battle;
He forces down the bow, unnerves the hand—
    rebels cannot muster strength for opposition;
He is hawk-eyed, skull-splitting—
    none make a stand near him.

"Wide striding, he shoots down the coward runaway—
    and there's an end to all who show their heels.
Unflinching under pressure of assault,
    he faces forward—never turns *his* back!
Steadfast he eyes the surging multitude
    and never lets the villains gain his center;
Eager, he harries the easterners,
    exulting, herds the barbarians.

"Let him but seize the shield to enter battle,
    he never need do twice the deed of devastation!
There are none who escape his arrow,
    none who can draw his bow.
Foreign cohorts flee before him
    as from the vengeance of the Mighty Goddess;
Fighting in his absence ends—
    he cannot linger for the stragglers.

"Yet he is dearly loved, deep in the people's affection,
    taking the throne as his own with their blessing:
His citizens treasure him more than their own flesh,
    set him above their own god.
They pass down the roadways singing with joy in him
    now he is king;

But he took this land while still with his mother,
　　　　his eye on the kingdom before he was born.

"He shall make Egypt's children be many and multiply,
　　　　yet he is one, the One given of God.
Egypt enjoys all he inherited—
　　　　now he shall broaden her far-flung borders:
He shall go forth and take the lands of the south,
　　　　never think twice of the northern nations;
He is sent by God to smite Asiatics
　　　　and grind the desert tribes into dust. . . .

"Write him! Make sure he knows your name!
　　　　And do not weigh the distance to his Majesty
　　　　　　　that he may help you as his father did.
He cannot fail to aid
　　　　a country asking his protection."

Amunenshi then replied,
　　　　"Egypt surely will be well;
　　　　　　　she knows his guiding hand. . . .
But you are here, so you shall stay with me;
　　　　and I shall do you good."

V I
And so he set me down, honored among his children,
　　　　and wed me to his oldest girl,
And let me have my choice of all his districts
　　　　picked from the very best of what was his
　　　　　　　up at the border with the neighboring country:
　　　　it was a lovely land, called Yaa.

Figs were there, along with grapevines:
　　　　wine flowed more plentiful than water.
A land of honey, endless with olives,
　　　　and fruits of every kind bent down its branches.

91

And there was barley there, and emmer;
      the land lay well, luxuriant with livestock.
Greatness and power indeed reached out to me
      because of his affection.

Then he set me to rule the people
      in that choicest and best of places.
They furnished me food day by day
      and wine was a daily pleasure,
With always cooked meat or roast duck
      or dishes of desert game.
They snared for me and they fished for me,
      swelling the catch of my own greyhounds;
And they filled me with numberless sweets,
      and milk and abundance of baked goods.

I spent untold years there;
      my sons grew to powerful men
          each leading his own people.
The envoy speeding north or south toward home—
      he stopped awhile with me.
Indeed, all mankind knew my courtesy:
      I gave the thirsty one to drink,
I set the lost upon his way,
      I succored him whom thieves had wrecked.

Now, the Asiatics fell to insurrection
      baiting rulers of the upland counties;
          and I was totally opposed to all their scheming.
So my good lord of Retenu,
      he had me spend more years
Acting as marshal of his forces;
      and each hill district flocked to me for refuge.

Then I swept down upon those Asian hordes,
      and doom descended on their wells and pastures.

I took their cattle,
    carried off their farmers;
I seized their harvests
    and I killed their people
With my strong arm, with my bow,
    my tactics and my skillful strategy.

I stood there expert in my master's heart, for he esteemed me;
    and now he knew that I was brave.
He made me foremost among all his offspring
    having seen my strong arm prosper.

VII

Then came a doughty chief of Retenu
    to taunt me, goad me from my tent;
He was supreme, a champion without contenders,
    since he had overmanned them, every one.
He said he wanted single combat with me
    fully expecting he would lay me low,
Intending to carry off my cattle
    under the evil urging of his tribe.

That other lord, my chief, he begged a word with me—
    I protesting that I did not know the man:
"I am certainly no friend of his
    that I could wander free in his encampment!
Does it look like I could force his private chamber
    having breached his wall and stormed his citadel?
He is beside himself because he sees me
    happily embarked on your affairs.

"Surely I am like the lead bull of a roving band
    chanced in the middle of a settled herd:
The hero of the native stock attacks him
    while other longhorns nudge and menace.
Is ever man of humble origin esteemed

in the capacity of master?
No desert wanderer joins with a Delta farmer!
And who would grow papyrus in the mountains?
Is there a bull aching to test the champion
who dares to sound retreat
for fear he might not equal him?
If this chief's lust be all to fight,
let him speak out what weighs upon his mind.
Can God be ignorant of what this man has planned?
The question is, my good lord, How can *we* know?"

I spent the night testing my bow,
cutting and truing arrows,
Made some practice passes with my dagger
and readied all my gear.

Day dawned; all Retenu was come,
for they had irritated and inflamed its peoples
And gathered districts sympathetic to their cause—
oh, they indeed had staged this confrontation!

He made his entrance there where I was standing,
for I had made myself available to him.
The thoughts of all burned fierce with anguish for me,
women and men murmured in alien tongues;
Each heart had pity on me, asking,
"Is there another hero able to do battle with him,
To stand against his shield, his axe,
his armful of such deadly missiles?"

Then I strode forth amidst his flying weaponry
which I let pass me harmless by:
His arrows bit thin air,
one following the other uselessly.
And then he made his sally
fully intending there to have me dead;

He neared me and I shot him,
     my arrow bedding in his neck;
He groaned, he fell upon his face,
     and I dispatched him with his battle-axe.

I roared my victory shout over his prostrate form
     while each vile Asian howled,
Gave thanks to Montu, Lord of battle,
     while his inept supporters wept for him.
Our friend and master, Amunenshi—
     he wrapped me in his arms.

At that I carried off this hero's goods
     and took his herds:
What he had planned to do to me
     I did to him.
I made my own whatever filled his tent
     and stripped his campsite bare.

Honor and power and glory were mine from that deed;
     only the far horizon bounded my heaped up riches;
          droves of my cattle, uncounted, covered the hills—
     thus does God ever act toward a man of goodwill:
He does not nurse anger against one
     who has wandered astray to the wrong land.

     And this day proves his heart is washed clean!

VIII

"A fugitive once fled his neighborhood;
     now word of me thunders back home.
One trusted to stay once crept away hungry;
     today I give bread to my neighbor.
A man abandoned his own land in nakedness;
     I am one who shines in fine linen.
A man went himself for want of a messenger;

I am a man rich in servants.
Splendid my tent here, and wide my domain—
　　　but I still have dreams of the palace.

"Lord of all gods, who ordered this flight,
　　　I pray you send me home!
Surely you will let me see
　　　the place my heart would dwell.
What better than my body's union
　　　with that earth where I was born?
Come, seek me out, that a good deed may be done,
　　　and let God give me peace.

"And may he act likewise
　　　to dignify the end of one he has afflicted;
May his heart pity one he has condemned
　　　to let life leak away on arid hills.
Is it today indeed that he is reconciled?
　　　Let him then hear the prayer of one afar!
Let the sojourner cease to range the land of his exile;
　　　let him go back to the country whence God brought him.

"And may the King of Egypt be at peace with me
　　　that I may live within the heartland of his mercy,
And greet my Lady who is in his palace,
　　　and hear tidings of her children.
Then would my very self grow young again!
　　　For now old age is come,
And misery, alone it drives me on;
　　　my eyelids fall, my arms are heavy,
　　　　　feet fail to follow the exhausted heart.

"O God, be near me for the final journey
　　　that they may guide me to the City of Forever
　　　　　to follow faithfully the Mistress of Us All.

Then would she tell me it is well with all her children,
   that she will while away eternity with me."

I X

At last it reached his Majesty's attention—
   He of the Sedge and the Bee, King Kheper-ka-re—
      about the state that my affairs were in.
And his Majesty sent such a message to me,
   accompanied by largesse of the Crown,
As warmed the heart of this his loyal subject
   like that of any ruler of a foreign country;
And each prince and princess in the palace with him
   made sure I heard their news.

Copy of the Order brought to this loyal subject
concerning his return to Egypt:

"The Horus, Life of the Dynasty,
   Two Ladies, Life of the Dynasty,
      Golden Horus, Life of the Dynasty,
He of the Sedge and the Bee, King Kheper-ka-re,
   Son of the Sun, Senusert,
      alive through worlds and time—
The Order of the King for my servant, Sinuhe:

"Item. This edict of the King is brought you
   to comment on your transmigration of the lands
      which go forth east from Qedem to the hills:

"Land gives you to land
   goaded by phantoms in your fevered brain.
What have you done that one should act against you?
   You did not blaspheme that your words should drive you off;
Nor did you ill-speak in the hall of elders

that your phrases should rise up to haunt you.
This foolish notion, it made you leave your senses!
        Nothing like that was ever in my heart against you.

"She, your Heaven in the palace, lives here still
        and flourishes today;
Her canopy of love is spread like sky, protecting earth;
        her children prosper in the audience chamber.
Now, be assured to have whatever they will give you
        that you may live henceforth on their affection.

"Make your return to Egypt
        to see once more the home wherein you grew,
To kiss your native earth before the towering Twin Doors,
        be reunited with my loyal Friends.

"By now old age is come upon you,
        manhood cut loose and drifts away;
So think today upon the day of burial,
        your passage into light:

"You shall be granted days of darkness with sweet oils,
        a linen shroud woven by gentle Taiyt's hands;
For you they slowly step the last cortege
        upon that day of mooring, union with the earth:
The coffin all of gold, the mask of heaven's blue,
        the very sky above you caught in the covered shrine;
Oxen draw and singers sing as they precede you,
        the dance for those at rest is danced at your last door;
For you they consecrate the funeral banquet
        and sacrifice is made upon your altars;
Your pillars rise, cut from the fine white limestone,
        close to the very bosom of my Family.

"No death of yours shall be on foreign soil,
        nor shall mere Asiatics make you earth;

Never shall you lie wrapped in a sheepskin
        that such might serve as your enclosure wall.
Death is duration longer than wandering this world;
        have care for your eternal body, and come home!"

X

This document arrived
        while I was standing there among my people.
It was read out to me,
        and I threw myself upon the ground
And gathered dust of earth,
        strewing it freely on my breast.
Then I strode back and forth through my encampment
        exulting, shouting out, and saying:
"How can this be done for a mere servant
        whose heart has gone astray to alien lands?
Oh, wonderful indeed the clemency of him
        who saves me from the hand of death.
It is your august Self, O King, that lets me make an end,
        my limbs at rest at home."

X I

Copy of the reply to this royal Edict.
Sinuhe, Servant of the Palace, says:

"With the utmost goodwill and submission
        regarding the matter of this exodus
                made by your loyal subject in his foolishness.
My greetings to you, beneficent god, Lord of the Two Lands,
        beloved of Re and favorite of Montu, Lord of Thebes.

"May Amun, Lord of the Throne of the Two Lands,
        and Sobek-Re, Horus, and Hathor,
Atum with his Ennead of gods,
        and Sopdu, Neferbau, Semseru, the Eastern Horus,
The Mistress of the Underworld (may She protect your brow),

the convocation of old deities upon the Waters,
And Min, and Horus of foreign lands,
    and the Great Goddess, Mistress of Punt,
And Nut, the Elder Horus, Re,
    and all the gods of Egypt and the Green Sea Islands—

"May they put breath of life into your nostrils,
    may they enrich you with their gifts,
And may they offer you eternity without an end
    and infinity unbounded.
May fear of you reverberate among the nations,
    and may all those beneath the round sun bow.

"This is the supplication of a servant to his Royal Master
    who can sustain him in the West:
The Lord of Understanding, who knows the common lot—
    he sees amid the awful majesty of Court
How this humbled servant fears to state his plea
    as when there is a matter of grave moment to report.

"But the great god, image of Re,
    himself makes wise the man who serves him;
And your loyal subject has in hand a small suggestion
    that One might take for his consideration:
Your Majesty is Horus, who seizes what he will—
    victorious your arms against all nations;
So, let your Majesty command
    that this your servant bring you back the prince of Qedem,
The chieftain of the Iawesh, south of Keshu,
    and the leader of the two Phoenician coastlands.
These are kings whose names are justly famous,
    come into prominence with high regard for you
(There is no need to mention Retenu,
    for it belongs to you like your own greyhounds).

"As for this flight made by your loyal subject:
    I did not plan it out beforehand,
        it never crossed my mind;
I did not fabricate or nurse it,
    nor do I know what tore me from the Throne.
It was like the twistings of a dream—
    as if a Delta man should find himself up-River
        or a bewildered marshman in the Nubian sand.

"I was not fearful; no one followed me;
    I did not hear a whisper of reproach;
Nor was my name proscribed by edict of the marshal
    so that vile worms should be the judges of my body.
But yet my feet moved fast, my feelings mastered me;
    and God, who destined flight, thus drove me on.
I was not ever one to disobey—
    a good man holds in awe the customs of his country;
And Re has set the fear of you throughout the world,
    dread of you pervades each foreign nation.

"I beg you, take me home!
    save me from all this!
For it is you who clothe this far horizon,
    the very sun disk shines because of you;
The water in the streams, its moisture is your love;
    the wind of heaven, its very breath your speaking.

"This loyal subject shall pass power to my fledglings
    whom I have gotten in this place:
Homecoming it shall be, as offered to your servant;
    and may your Majesty do as you will.
One lives upon the breath of your dispensing,
    beloved of Re, of Horus, and of Hathor;
Your very nostrils, they signify our riches,
    O you whom Montu, Lord of Thebes eternal, loves."

XII

They let me spend a day in Yaa
　　　　transferring my possessions to my offspring;
My oldest son was set to lead my people,
　　　　and all my property left in his hand—
My serfs, my many herds,
　　　　my vines, and all my orchards.

So then this servant journeyed south toward home,
　　　　halting at Fort Horusways;
And the commander there, who led the border watch,
　　　　forwarded a message to the Residence
　　　　　　　in order that the King might be informed.

His Majesty dispatched the Minister of Planters,
　　　　a skillful man devoted to the royal House;
And heavy-laden ships came after him
　　　　bringing largesse of the Crown
Meant for those Asiatics who returned with me
　　　　conducting me to Horusways.
I said good-bye to each of them by name
　　　　while each gift-bearing servant did them honor.
Then I took to hoisting sail—
　　　　with beer and baked provisions by my side—
　　　　　　　until I reached the wharf at home.

XIII

Next day the dawn came early to the earth,
　　　　and summons came for me—
Ten men arriving, ten men going forth
　　　　escorting me in triumph to the palace.
I offered head to ground before the statues of the Children
　　　　which towered in the gateway, greeting me.
Courtiers attending in the outer hall
　　　　showed me directly to the audience chamber.

I found his Majesty upon the Throne of Egypt
       in the throne room all of silvered gold.
Really there, at last, before him,
       I stretched myself full length upon the floor;
But then my foolish brain turned witless in his presence,
       just as this god was offering warm welcome.
I was a man seized in the grip of darkness—
       my bird-soul flown, my limbs unstrung;
My heart, no longer was it in my body
       so that I might distinguish life from death.

Then said his Majesty to an attendant courtier,
       "Raise him. Let him speak with me."
And then he said, "Well, well, you have come home,
       done wandering the weary world since your departure!
I see the marks of time etched on your body;
       you have grown old.
When death must come, your rites shall not be wanting—
       your burial shall never be by bedouin tribes.
Now, deprecate yourself no longer:
       you spoke no treason; your name is honored here."

But still I was afraid of punishment
       and answered with the answer of a frightened man,
"What is it I have said, my Lord?
       Then I could speak to it.
It was no deed of mine;
       it was the hand of God:
Fear surged throughout my body
       as if to force a flight divinely ordered. . . .

"But let that be.
       I stand here in your presence;
    to you my life belongs;
       and may your Majesty do with me what you will."

Then he had the royal Family ushered in,
    and his Majesty said to the Queen,
"Look, here we have Sinuhe
    come back pure Semite, transformed into an Asian."

At that she uttered an astounded, "No!"
    and the Children all put forth a mock-believing gasp,
Exclaiming to his Majesty,
    "Surely it is not he, our sovereign Lord?"
        The King, "It surely is."

Then the princesses put on their beads of supplication
    and with scepters and their sistra in their hands
        made presentation of a song to please his Majesty:

"Your state is more than royal, O King,
    shining with the glory of the Queen of Heaven.
The Golden One gives life unto your nostrils,
    and the Lady of the Stars protects you;
White Crown travels north, and Red fares south,
    joined in everlasting union in your Person;
        the Serpent rears herself upon your brow.

"You have delivered humblest men from evil,
    gratifying Re, Lord of our Land:
        praises to you, as to the Mistress of Us All!
Lower your bow, unstring your arrow;
    give breath to one who is in need of air!
Grant us this special gift
    in favor of our errant guide, Son of the Northwind,
        this bedouin born in our beloved Land.
He ran away for fear of you,
    he left the land in terror of you;
And yet no face should pale at seeing yours,
    no fear unman the eye that looks to you."

And then his Majesty replied, "He shall not fear henceforth
    that he should falter so from terror.
He shall have rank as Royal Friend among my counselors,
    be placed within the inmost circle of the Court.
Proceed now to the dressing chamber
    to be of service to him."

Oh, what a Coming Forth it was for me that day—
    it was like resurrection—out of that royal hall!
The Children offered me their arms
    and then we went, together, out the Double Doors.

XIV

I stayed at a prince's estate amid riches long lost to me:
    a cool reception hall, scenes of the life hereafter,
Masterpieces from the Treasury,
    soft-woven garments, and perfumes of delicate fragrance.
Counselors the King esteemed lived in the rooms,
    and every servant went about his duties.

They made the years fall from my body:
    I was taken and sheared, and my hair combed,
And a heavy load was given to the sandy hills—
    the cast-off livery of a desert wanderer;
I was appareled in the finest linen,
    anointed with the sweetest-smelling oils,
        and put to rest at night upon a real bed.
I bequeathed the sand to those who lived in it
    and the oil of tree to him who smelled of it.

I received a nobleman's plantation
    as befitting one who ranked as Royal Friend.
A company of expert craftsmen readied it,
    and all its woodwork was restored like new;
Food was sent me from the palace

three and even four times every day—
     not counting what the royal Children gave.
And not one moment did these wonders cease!

There was made for me a pyramid of stone
     built in the shadow of the royal Tomb.
The god's own masons hewed the blocks for it,
     and its walls were portioned out among them;
The draftsman and the painter drew in it,
     the master sculptor carved;
The overseer of workmen at the tombs
     crisscrossed the length of Egypt on account of it.
Implements and furniture were fitted in its storeroom
     and all that would be needful brought within;
Servants for my Spirit were appointed,
     a garden was laid out above,
And tended fields ran downward to the village—
     just as is ordered for a nearest Friend.
My statue was all brushed with burnished gold,
     its kilt set off with silver.

It was his Majesty who did all this for me.
     No simple man has ever had so much.
And I enjoyed the sunshine of his royal favor
     until my day of mooring dawned.

This was its unfolding,
beginning to end,
as found in writing.

APPENDIX A

Sources of the Texts

"Man dies, his body is dust" (epigraph)

Pap. Chester Beatty IV = Pap. British Museum 10684, vso 3.3-5. In Alan H. Gardiner, ed., *Hieratic Papyri in the British Museum*. 3rd series. 2 vols. Chester Beatty Gift (London: British Museum, 1935).

From the Conclusion to *The Instruction for Merikare* (p. 3)

Pap. Leningrad 1116A, Pap. Moscow 4658, and Pap. Carlsberg VI. Cf. W. Golénischeff, *Les papyrus hiératiques nos. 1115, 1116A et 1116B de l'Hermitage Impérial à St. Petersburg* (St. Petersburg, 1913). Most conveniently read in W. Helck, *Die Lehre für Merikare*, Kleine ägyptische Texte (Wiesbaden: Otto Harrassowitz, 1977), pp. 77–87.

Akhenaten's Hymn to the Sun (p. 5)

N. de G. Davies, *The Rock Tombs of el Amarna*. Vol. 6, *Archeological Survey of Egypt, Eighteenth Memoir* (London: Egypt Exploration Fund, 1907; reprint 1975), pl. 27.

The Debate Between a Man Tired of Life and His Soul (p. 11)

Pap. Berlin 3024. Hieratic text best read in Hans Goedicke, *The Report about the Dispute of a Man with His Ba* (Baltimore and London: Johns Hopkins University Press, 1970). Transcriptions: *idem*. and R. O. Faulkner, "The Man Who Was Tired of Life," *Journal of Egyptian Archaeology* 42 (1956), 22–26.

The Resurrection of King Ounas (p. 19)

Tomb of Unis (or Ounas): Pyramid Texts, Utterances 273–74. In Kurt Sethe, ed., *Die Altägyptischen Pyramidentexte*, vol. 1 (Leipzig: J. C. Hinrichs Verlag, 1908; reprint 1969), pp. 205–16.

The Tale of the Shipwrecked Sailor (p. 24)

Pap. Leningrad 1115. In W. Golénischeff, *Les papyrus hiératique nos. 1115, 1116A, et 1116B de l'Hermitage Impérial à St. Petersburg* (St. Petersburg, 1913). Transcription: Aylward M. Blackman, *Middle Egyptian Stories*, pt. 1, Bibliotheca Aegyptiaca 2 (Brussels: La Fondation Égyptologique Reine Élisabeth, 1931), pp. 41–48.

Spell for Causing the Beloved to Follow After (p. 32)

Deir el-Medineh Ostracon 1057. In G. Posener, *Catalogue des ostraca hiératique littéraire de Deir el Médineh*, tome 1 (Cairo: L'Institut français d'archéologie orientale, 1938), pls. 31, 31a.

Spell for Power from the Four Winds of Heaven (p. 33)

Coffin Texts, Spell 162. In Adriaan de Buck, *The Egyptian Coffin Texts*, vol. 2 (Chicago: University of Chicago Press, 1938), pp. 389–405.

The Testament of Amenemhat, King of Egypt (p. 36)

In Jesús López, "Le Papyrus Millingen," *Revue d'égyptologie* 15 (1963), 29–33 and pls. 4–8, as well as many other papyri and ostraca. Fullest transcription in W. Helck, *Der Text der 'Lehre Amenemhats I. für seinen Sohn,'* Kleine ägyptische Texte (Wiesbaden: Otto Harrassowitz, 1969). Also: J. Foster, "The Conclusion to 'The Testament of Ammenemes, King of Egypt,'" *Journal of Egyptian Archaeology* 67 (1981), 36–47 and pls. 4–11.

Hymn to Osiris (p. 40)

Stele of Amenmose, Louvre C. 286. In A Moret, "La légend d'Osiris, *Bulletin de l'Institut français d'Archéologie Orientale* 30 (1931), 725–30 and pls. 1–3.

Hymn to the Nile (p. 47)

Papyri Turin 1968 + 1890 + 1878, Pap. Anastasi VII, Pap. Chester Beatty V, Pap. Sallier II, and numerous ostraca. Best read in D. van der Plas, *L'Hymne a la crue du Nil*, 2 vols. (Leiden: Nederlands Instituut voor het Nabije Oosten, 1986).

From *The Maxims of Ptahhotep* (p. 53)

Pap. Prisse and others. Facsimile: G. Jéquier, *Le papyrus Prisse et ses variantes* (Paris, 1911). Transcription of the main papyri: Z. Žaba, *Les maximes de Ptahhotep* (Prague, 1956), esp. pp. 15–21.

Menna's Lament, or Letter to a Wayward Son (p. 56)

Oriental Institute Chicago Ostracon 12074. Translated directly from the ostracon. Facsimile and transcription in J. Černý and A. Gardiner, *Hieratic Ostraca*, vol. 1 (Oxford: Griffith Institute, 1957), pls. 78–79a.

Lament to Amun (p. 59)

Pap. Anastasi IV, 10.1–5. In A. Gardiner, *Late-Egyptian Miscellanies* (Brussels: La Fondation Égyptoligique Reine Élisabeth, 1937), p. 45.

Longing for Memphis (p. 60)

Pap. Anastasi IV, 4.10–5.5. In A. Gardiner, *Late-Egyptian Miscellanies* (Brussels: La Fondation Égyptologique Reine Élisabeth, 1937), p. 39.

For a Portrait of the Queen in Luxor Temple (p. 61)

Luxor Temple, Court of Ramesses II, West Wall, North of Doorway. Cf. Bertha Porter and Rosalind L. B. Moss, *Topographical Bibliography of Ancient Egyptian Hieroglyphic Texts, Reliefs, and Paintings.* Vol. 2, *Theban Temples* (2nd ed.), (Oxford: Clarendon Press, 1972), p. 308 (å28: III). Text taken from translator's hand copy.

From *The Leiden Hymns* (p. 63)

Pap. Leiden I 350. Transcription in J. Zandee, *De Hymnen aan Amon van Papyrus Leiden I 350* (Leiden: Rijksmuseum van Oudheden, 1947), esp. Bijlage 1, "Hieroglyphische Tekst," pls. 1–6.

The Harper's Song for Inherkhawy (p. 80)

Deir el-Medineh Tomb 359, Wall 11, Register 3, Scene 17. Facsimile in B. Bruyère, *Fouilles de l'Institut français* 8 (Cairo: L'Institut français d'archéologie orientale, 1930), p. 70 and pl. 23.

From *The Eloquent Peasant* (p. 82)

Papyri Berlin 3023, 3025, and 10499, and Pap. British Museum 10274. The first three appear in F. Vogelsang and A. Gardiner, *Die Klagen des Bauern, Literarische Texte aus den Mittleren Reiches 1.* Vol. 4, *Hieratische Papyrus aus den Königlichen Museen zu Berlin* (Leipzig: J. Hinrichs, 1908; reprint 1970).

The Tale of Sinuhe (p. 85)

Papyri Berlin 3022 and 10499; Ashmolean Ostracon of *Sinuhe;* and several fragmentary ostraca and pieces of papyrus. Cf. A. Gardiner, *Die Erzählung des Sinuhe und Die Hirtengeschichte, Literarische Texte des Mittleren Reiches 2. Vol. 5, Hieratische Papyrus aus den Königlichen Museen zu Berlin* (Leipzig: J. Hinrichs, 1909; reprint 1970). Also: J. Barns, *The Ashmolean Ostracon of Sinuhe* (Oxford: Griffith Institute, 1952). A parallel text transcription in A. Blackman, *Middle-Egyptian Stories*, pt. I, Bibliotheca Aegyptiaca 2 (Brussels: La Fondation Égyptoligique Reine Élisabeth, 1932).

Chronology

Thinite Period	Dynasties I–II	ca. 3030–2665 B.C.
Old Kingdom	Dynasty III	ca. 2665–2600 B.C.
	Dynasty IV	ca. 2600–2480 B.C.
	Dynasty V	ca. 2480–2320 B.C.
	Dynasty VI	ca. 2320–2155 B.C.
First Intermediate Period	Dynasties VII–VIII	ca. 2155–2135 B.C.
	Dynasties IX–XI	ca. 2134–2040 B.C.
Middle Kingdom	Dynasty XI	ca. 2040–1991 B.C.
	Dynasty XII	ca. 1991–1785 B.C.
	Dynasty XIII	ca. 1785–1650 B.C.
Second Intermediate Period	Dynasties XIV–XVII	ca. 1650–1551 B.C.
New Kingdom	Dynasty XVIII	ca. 1551–1305 B.C.
	Dynasties XIX–XX	ca. 1305–1080 B.C.
Third Intermediate Period	Dynasties XXI–XXV	ca. 1080–655 B.C.
Late Period	Dynasties XXVI–XXXI	ca. 664–332 B.C.
Ptolemaic Period		ca. 332–30 B.C.
Roman Province		ca. 30 B.C.–330 A.D.

SOURCE: After J. von Beckerath, *Abriss der Geschichte des alten Agypten* (Munich-Wien: R. Oldenbourg, 1971).

APPENDIX C

A Note to the Specialist

I have not used the so-called second tenses or emphatic forms in my translations because they often seem either irrelevant or downright inimical to the sense I find in a given passage. I am not sure such forms actually occur, at least in Middle Egyptian verse texts. I realize that almost no other student of the ancient Egyptian language agrees with me on this point.

Nor have I employed the convention of signaling gaps in the original text by a series of dots or by brackets or parentheses. Such conventions (very proper in literal translations) destroy mood and tone in literary translations. I have not knowingly anywhere supplied words that were not either present or clearly implied in the originals as I have read and interpreted them. Specialists may check my texts and choices by referring to the finding list above (appendix A).

Glossary

Abydos. Very ancient Egyptian city north of Thebes, seat of the kings of Dynasties I and II (the Thinite Period) and prime religious center of Egypt, home of the worship of Osiris.

Admonitions. A subcategory of instruction or didactic literature ("wisdom texts") warning against moral and social evils.

Adversary, the. See **Apophis.**

Akhenaten, King. Monotheist king of later Dynasty XVIII. Reigned 1365–1347 B.C. He worshipped a single god, the Aten, denying the existence, or at least the worship, of the other gods, and initiating profound changes in Egyptian religion and art. His religion did not outlast him.

Amenemhat I, King. First king of Dynasty XII, toward the beginning of the Middle Kingdom. Reigned 1991–1962 B.C.

Amun. The Hidden One, King of the Gods. An ancient god, but rising into prominence at Thebes during Dynasty XI and throughout the Middle Kingdom to become the great cosmic, imperial, and universal god of New Kingdom Egypt.

Amun-Re. Became the full name of Amun (see previous entry) as that god absorbed the power and functions of the earlier sun and creator god of Heliopolis.

Amunenshi. Ruler of Upper Retenu in twentieth-century B.C. Syria-Palestine; appears in *The Tale of Sinuhe.*

Andjeti. Ancient god worshipped in the Delta and a precursor of Osiris, into whose nature he blends.

Anglo-Saxon. Also called Old English (450–1100 A.D.).

Antagonist, the. See **Apophis.**

Anubis. God of the dead, of embalming, and of the necropolis. The prime funerary god before the rise of Osiris.

Apophis. Cosmic serpent demon who attacked the sun god's (Re's) barque each night, thus endangering the cosmic order. Defeated each night, he was reborn each day. One of the fixed elements in the universe, symbolizing chaos; hence, the (Great) Antagonist or the Adversary of the sun god.

Asheru. The sacred lake and divine precinct about the Temple of Mut at Karnak in ancient Thebes.

Asiatics. Peoples to the northeast of Egypt in Syria-Palestine and Mesopotamia (the Fertile Crescent in general).

Aten. (also **Aton**). Sun god symbolized by the disk of the sun. Became the sole god during the reign of Akhenaten in the fourteenth century B.C..

117

Atum. The Old One and Lord of the Ennead. An early version of the sun god and creator of the universe. The center of his worship lay at Heliopolis. Succeeded in his functions by Re, also of Heliopolis.

Ba. An aspect of the personality, according to the ancient Egyptians. Continuing after death and often described or depicted in the form of a bird. The closest approximation (but not an exact equivalent) is our word "soul."

Barque of Re. The ship in which the sun god travels at night to move through the darkness from the West to the East to begin the new day.

Bee. Emblem of Lower Egypt. See **He of the Sedge and the Bee.**

Beginning, the. The Egyptian term for the moment or time of creation, the "First Occasion" or the "First Day." The account takes various forms but describes the emergence of order from chaos. The primary account has the creator god appearing on a primal hill that emerges from the midst of the primeval waters and on which he stands to accomplish the work of creation.

Belles-lettres. Literature as works of art—for ancient Egypt, consisting primarily of tales and myths, various types of instructional or didactic material ("wisdom texts"), complaints and laments, hymns, prayers, and love songs. Not literature in the broader sense of anything written down.

Black Land. A common name for Egypt, referring to the black of the fertile soil as opposed to the red of the sterile desert.

Busiris. Ancient city in the central Delta. In religious traditions the home of Osiris. The name derives from *Pr Wsir*, "the House of Osiris."

Byblos. Very ancient city on the eastern Mediterranean coast of what is now Lebanon. There was Egyptian contact with it from the earliest dynasties.

Cartouche. The oval within which were written the fourth and fifth names (the prenomen and nomen) in the royal titulary.

Champollion, Jean François (1790–1832). Deciphered the Egyptian hieroglyphic writing in 1822.

Chaos. The condition of things before creation of the universe by the sun god. Conceived of as a turmoil of water, wind, and darkness. The chaos was believed to continue outside the formed universe, and such beings as Apophis try to force a return to the original state of disorder.

Chaucer, Geoffrey (ca. 1343–1400). Most famous poet writing in the Middle English stage of the English language.

Children, the. The royal offspring of both sexes, at least in *The Tale of Sinuhe*.

City of Sun. Heliopolis, center of worship of the sun god.

Coffin Texts. Religious texts consisting mainly of spells to aid the deceased that were carved or painted on the coffins of nobles from Dynasty XI to XVII. They had a wider range of themes and subject matter than the Pyramid Texts, which were limited to kings and queens.

Coming Forth. Literally, the ability of the deceased's spirit to emerge from the tomb after death to enjoy the benefits of this world. A kind of resurrection, especially for Sinuhe after his reception by the king after the living death of his lifetime exile.

Coptic. The final phase of the ancient Egyptian language (from the third century A.D. on), written in the Greek alphabet with additional characters derived from the hieroglyphs. The only stage of the Egyptian language to write out the vowels. Coptic was gradually replaced by Arabic after the Arab Conquest in A.D. 640.

Craftsman, the. Epithet for the god Ptah in his function as inventor of crafts and protector of artisans.

Creator God. The first god and the one who created the universe from chaos. In various versions of the myth and over the long span of Egyptian history, he was the cosmic Horus, Atum, Re, Ptah, Amun, and Amun-Re.

David, King. Israelite king of the United Monarchy. Reigned circa 1000–961 B.C.

Death the Crocodile. Personification of the moment of death as being seized and devoured by crocodiles lurking in the Nile. An unpleasant way to die.

Deir el-Medineh. Village of the craftsmen and artists who decorated the rock-cut royal tombs in the Valley of the Kings during the New Kingdom. Excavation of a trash pit there has uncovered thousands of ostraca, many with portions of the classic literature of ancient Egypt.

Delta. The northern portion of Egypt (north of modern Cairo) where the Nile River fans out to empty into the Mediterranean Sea. Also called Lower Egypt.

Demotic. A very cursive form of the hieratic writing of the ancient Egyptian language used in books and documents primarily from Dynasty XXV to the Roman period (from 715 B.C. to 470 A.D.).

Diodorus Siculus. Roman historian, flourishing under Caesar and Augustus (ca. 60–30 B.C.), wrote a multivolume world history, the first book of which dealt with Egypt.

Djoser (Zoser), King. Ruled during Dynasty III (ca. 2650–2630 B.C.). Owner of the Step Pyramid at Saqqara, the world's first monumental building made of stone.

Dynasty. Term used to designate a coherent succession of Egyptian rulers, usually a "royal house," that is, several generations of one family succeeding to the throne, son after father. In actuality the succession was not this neat. Nevertheless, Manetho used this principle to divide the historical span of ancient Egypt into thirty-one such dynasties. See appendix B, "Chronology," for a list of these dynasties.

Eastern Horus, the. The cosmic Horus as lord of lands east of Egypt. Possibly Horakhty, "Horus of the Two Horizons," where the sun rose and set.

Elder Horus, the. The ancient cosmic sky and sun god, known from earliest dynastic times; depicted as a falcon (whose eyes were the sun and the moon). Not the child Horus, son of Isis and Osiris.

Eight Great Gods (Ogdoad). The Eight Great Gods personifying elements of the chaos preceding creation of the world, according to the traditions of Hermopolis. They existed in male-female pairs and were Nun and Naunet (the primitive watery abyss), Heh and Hehet (infinite space), Kek and Keket (darkness), and Amun and Amaunet (invisibility or hidden power.)

Elohist, the (fl. ca. 850 B.C.). Anonymous Israelite writer who composed the northern version (Ephraimite) of the traditions of Israel.

119

Ennead (Nine Great Gods). The original generations of gods according to the cosmogony of Heliopolis. The creator god, Atum, without consort fathered Shu (air or space) and Tefnut (moisture), whose children were Nut (sky) and Geb (earth). Their offspring were the Osirian family: Osiris, Isis, Nephthys, and Seth. Later, the child Horus (different from the cosmic Horus) was added as born to Isis after Seth murdered Osiris.

Eye of Re. The royal uraeus, a serpent goddess, sometimes personified by either Hathor or Sakhmet as agents of Re's judgment or vengeance, often carrying out the punishment of evildoers, such as humankind when it plotted to rebel against Re.

Ezekiel. (fl. ca. 593–573 B.C.). Biblical prophet during the Exile, when the Children of Israel (actually, of Judah) were conquered by King Nebuchadnezzar of Babylon and deported (ca. 597 B.C.) to the city of Babylon, where they remained until Cyrus of Persia took Babylon in 539 B.C. and allowed the exiles to return to their homeland. These events took place during Dynasty XXVI.

Falcon. Form of the cosmic sky god and royal god, Horus.

Falcon, the. Specifically referring to the king as earthly embodiment of the cosmic Horus while on the throne of Egypt.

Fashioner, the. An epithet for Ptah, the divine artisan and craftsman.

First Day. See **Beginning, the.**

First Intermediate Period. See appendix B, "Chronology."

Fort Horusways. Fort on the northeastern border guarding the main road from Egypt to Syria-Palestine and Asia.

Geb. Earth god, according to the Heliopolitan cosmogony. Consort of Nut, the sky, and father of Osiris, Isis, Nephthys, and Seth.

Giza. Northern end of the great Memphite necropolis and site of the pyramids of Khufu, Khaefre, and Menkaure (or, in the Greek spelling, Cheops, Chephren, and Mycerinus) as well as the Sphinx and many mastaba tombs of the Old Kingdom nobility.

God. A deity, or the ultimate deity. Egyptian religion was polytheistic except during the reign of Akhenaten, who was a monotheist. However, in individual hymns and prayers, and profoundly in *The Leiden Hymns*, the singular ("God") is used as if no other deity existed for the duration of the hymn or prayer. In *The Leiden Hymns* the theological problem of the many in the one is specifically addressed so as to make the ultimate godhead apparently monotheistic, with the other gods as incarnations or variant forms of the ultimate deity. Some scholars prefer to describe the Egyptians under Akhenaten as "henotheists" rather than "monotheists."

Golden Horus. Designation for the third of the five names in the royal titulary.

Golden One, the. Epithet of Hathor, especially in her capacity as goddess of love.

Great Cackler, the. Form of the creator god (here, Amun) as a goose or falcon that creates the world by laying a great cosmic egg. Also known as the Shrieker.

Great Goddess, the. Epithet of various goddesses, perhaps in some contexts as a kind of mother-goddess.

Great Green Sea. Usually the Mediterranean Sea but sometimes apparently the Red

Sea (as in "The Tale of the Shipwrecked Sailor"). Probably, its root meaning is "the open sea."

Great Salt Sea. Probably the marshy area of the eastern Delta, where Sinuhe wandered on his way to Syria-Palestine.

Ha. God of the desert regions (and oases) west of the Nile Valley and Delta.

Handsome of Face, the. Epithet for Ptah of Memphis.

Hapy. God of the Nile inundation. Not so much the river itself as the energy of renewal and fertility that returned each year with the overflowing of the Nile.

Harper's songs. A kind of poem, funerary and generally found in tombs, chanted by a harper (often blind) sitting before the deceased owner (or owners) of the tomb. The theme of these songs was the finality of death; they urged the living to "seize the day," to enjoy life while it lasted, for tomorrow it would be gone. The type seems very un-Egyptian yet is found on walls right next to traditional poems and spells extolling the joys of the afterlife.

Harpist. One version of the ancient Egyptian lyric poet or performer. He appears not only in the harper's songs but also helps provide music in the company of other musicians, singers, and dancers at banquets of the living.

Hathor. Ancient goddess often represented in cow form. In some myths she is the mother of the king, while her usual function is as either a funerary goddess or the goddess of love, music, and dancing.

Hathors, the Seven. Goddesses of fate acting collectively and determining the destiny of a child at birth.

He of the Sedge and the Bee. Referring to the king, especially to his prenomen (the fourth name of his royal titulary), as the one belonging to the Sedge of Upper Egypt (the Valley) and to the Bee of Lower Egypt (the Delta) and thus uniting the Two Lands.

Hedj-hetep. God of weaving.

Heliopolis. Ancient city northeast (and now a suburb) of Cairo. Center of worship of the sun and creator god, primarily as Re but also as Atum, Khepri, and Re-Horakhty. Source of the theology of the Ennead.

Heracleopolis. City just south of the Fayyum. Capital of Dynasties IX–X and setting for a number of classic pieces of Middle Egyptian literature, such as *The Instruction for Merikare* and *The Eloquent Peasant.*

Hermopolis. City about midway between ancient Memphis and Thebes. Center for the worship of Thoth and source of the theology of the Ogdoad, the Eight Great Gods.

Herodotus. Greek historian who visited Egypt about 450 B.C. Egypt is treated in Book 2 of his *Histories.*

Hieratic. The cursive form of the ancient Egyptian language adapted for rapid writing by reed pen and ink on papyrus, pottery, or stone. It uses the same signs as the hieroglyphs, but much abbreviated.

Hieroglyphic. The original forms of the signs of the ancient Egyptian language in pictorial form. The difference between hieroglyphic and hieratic writing is roughly analogous to that between block printing and handwriting. Originally used for carving signs into stone by means of a chisel.

121

Horus. One of the oldest and most complex gods of the Egyptian pantheon. Originally a sky god in the shape of a falcon, he has three primary forms: (1) the cosmic Horus, the sky god; (2) Horus as incarnated in the reigning king of Egypt, the pharaoh; and (3) Horus the child, son of Osiris and Isis. Other forms of Horus seem to be manifestations of these three.

Horus, the. First name of the royal titulary, signifying the king as an incarnation of Horus, first as the cosmic deity, but also as the child of, and successor on the throne to, his deceased royal predecessor, who at death was assimilated into Osiris.

Horus of Foreign Lands. Probably the cosmic Horus as lord and protector of foreign lands.

Horus of Twin Horizons. Horakhty. The cosmic Horus as sun god of the East and West, the two horizons where the sun rises and sets. Seen usually as a separate god and primarily of the sunrise.

Hymn. A major genre of ancient Egyptian literature. A poem in praise of or worshipping a deity, the divine king, or on occasion a city (Thebes) or an object (the personified Red or White Crowns of Egypt). Its purpose is homage.

Hypselis. City in Middle Egypt mentioned in "The Great Hymn to Osiris" as a center of his worship.

Iaaw. Father of the god of the western desert, Ha, but otherwise unidentified.

Iawesh. Possibly a people or a place, whose chieftains Sinuhe offers to bring back to his sovereign, King Senusert I.

Inherkhawy. Owner of Tomb 359 at Deir el-Medineh in Western Thebes. He was Chief of Workmen in the Place of Truth (i.e., the necropolis). He lived during the reigns of Ramesses III and IV and was buried circa 1160 B.C.

Instructions. The prime didactic genre of ancient Egyptian literature. These teachings are usually cast as the wisdom of a father, who has led a public life, which is being passed on orally as a series of maxims to a son so as to prepare him in turn for government service.

Inundation. The annual overflowing of the Nile, bringing new silt for the farmer's fields and making life in Egypt possible.

Isis. Great mother goddess, daughter of Geb, sister and wife of Osiris, and mother of Horus. In the Osirian legend, after the murder of her husband by Seth, she searches for the pieces of his dismembered body, resurrects him, and bears his posthumously conceived son, Horus, who upon his majority appeals to the great Ennead of gods for his rightful inheritance, the land of Egypt, which is then granted him by the divine tribunal.

Isle of Flame. A locality in the otherworld. Or, also, the original hillock in the midst of the primeval waters on which the sun god came into being.

Izezi (Isesi), King. Penultimate king of Dynasty V, reigning circa 2380–2340 B.C. Served by the famous vizier Ptahhotep.

Judges. Public officials who heard cases and offered judgments from the earliest times. They also acted collectively as the *qenbet*, the council of elders, whether at the local, nome, or national level.

Ka. An aspect of the personality as envisioned by the ancient Egyptians. Like the concept of the *ba*, it has no counterpart today. It represents something like the "vital energy" of the universe, particularly as embodied in a person, and thus implies creative force or the sustainment of life. The deceased is said to "go to his *ka*" when he dies.

Kamutef. Epithet of Amun, "Bull-of-his-Mother," as the god of procreative force and sexual fertility.

Keshu. Possibly a location in Syria-Palestine. From *The Tale of Sinuhe.*

Kheper-ka-re, King. The prenomen, or fourth name in the royal titulary, of King Senusert I, second king of Dynasty XII. Reigned approximately 1971–1926 B.C.

Khepri. A form of the creator sun god, represented in the form of a scarab beetle, imaged especially as the sun god at dawn rising from the eastern horizon and pushing the sun's disk across the sky. In one myth the sun god was Khepri in the morning, Re at noon, and Atum (the old one) going down to the western horizon at sunset.

Khety. Author of Dynasty XII, who is credited with writing the "Hymn to the Nile," "The Testament of Amenemhat, King of Egypt," and "The Satire on the Trades." He is called by a New Kingdom scribe "the best of them all." Not to be confused with King Khety of Dynasty X, who wrote *The Instruction for Merikare.*

Khety III Nebkaure, King. Probable author of *The Instruction for Merikare,* and predecessor of that king at Heracleopolis during Dynasty X. Reigned during the twenty-first century B.C.

Khonsu. Moon god, especially prominent at Thebes, where he is considered the child of Mut and Amun, thus completing the holy family of Thebes.

Khnum. The god manifested as a ram, a potter god who created and shaped life on the potter's wheel. He controlled the annual inundation of the Nile from what was then its presumed source at Elephantine in the south of Egypt.

Khor. Syria.

King of Upper and Lower Egypt. Appelation for the king, using his prenomen or fourth name in the royal titulary and emphasizing his dominion over both the Delta and the Nile Valley to the south.

Kush. The foreign land to the south of Egypt; present-day Sudan.

Lady of Red Peak. "Goddess of the Red Mountain," of the Gebel el-Ahmar northeast of Cairo in the neighborhood of Heliopolis. Site of a quarry operating during the Old Kingdom and later.

Lady of the Stars. Possibly Nut, the sky goddess.

Lady of Waters. Here, Neith, ancient goddess of Sais with various functions and legends. Mother of Sobek as creator god and the Ennead in the "Hymn to the Nile."

Lake of Death. Symbol for death as occurring in crocodile-infested waters.

Lapis lazuli. Mineral of bluish or bluish-green color, not native to ancient Egypt, used as a gemstone.

Laments. Or "complaints." A subcategory of ancient Egyptian literature, belonging primarily to the didactic genre, in which the author expresses grief and mourns over some state of affairs. See, for example, *The Lamentations of Ipu-wer* or "The Complaints of Kha-kheper-re-soneb."

Land of Papyri. An epithet for Lower Egypt or the Delta. See also **He of the Sedge and the Bee.**

Land of Sedge. An epithet for Upper Egypt, the Nile Valley. See also **He of the Sedge and the Bee.**

Late Egyptian. The stage of the Egyptian language comprising the vernacular of Dynasties XVIII–XXIV (ca. 1570–700 B.C.). Used for literary texts during the New Kingdom and later, but usually mixed with forms from the classical Middle Egyptian stage of the language except in business documents and letters.

Leiden. City in The Netherlands. The rich collection of the museum there includes Pap. Leiden I 350, which contains New Kingdom hymns from the time of Ramesses II called *The Leiden Hymns.*

Letopolis. City in the lower Western Delta north of Giza. Referred to in the "Hymn to Osiris" as a cult center for that god.

Libyan desert. The desert area west of Egypt.

Literal translation. A translation that is essentially a word-for-word carryover from one language to another, respecting the word order of the original and using the root or denotative meanings of the original vocabulary. It does not mean to, or attempt to, emphasize the aesthetic values inherent in the original text.

Literary translation. A translation that, building upon an accurate literal translation, attempts to present the original as a work of art. It emphasizes nuances of words, word echoes, patterns of images and comparisons, tone or mood in the work, sound harmonies and dissonances, characterization, setting, poetic form and genre, and all the devices that transform a "text" into a "poem" or other piece of literature.

Lord of Ma'at. Or "Lord of Justice." In *The Eloquent Peasant* refers to Re as creator and regulator of the universe. *Ma'at* includes our concepts of justice, truth, goodness, and universal harmony.

Lord of the Two Lands. Epithet of the king of Egypt.

Lord of the Universe. Epithet usually referring to the creator and sun god Re.

Lords of Truth. The Ennead of gods in the "Hymn to Osiris" sitting as a divine tribunal in judgment between the claims of Horus and Seth.

Lower Egypt. Northern Egypt above modern Cairo; the Delta.

Luxor. The modern city that partially overlies ancient Thebes on the east bank of the Nile.

Luxor Temple. New Kingdom temple toward the south of modern Luxor, built primarily by Amenhotep III (1403–1365 B.C.), with additions by Tutankhamun (1346–1336 B.C.), and with later major additions by Ramesses II (1290–1224 B.C.).

Ma'at. One of the most fundamental concepts of ancient Egyptian civilization. It is too broad and too extensive a concept to be translated by any one word; but it designates a combination of our concepts of justice, truth, goodness, and harmony, the last especially in the sense of cosmic harmony or order in the universe.

Creation occurred according to its principle; the pharaoh must rule under its auspices; and people must live by its dictates.

Maaty Canal. One of the first localities (somewhere south of Saqqara) mentioned by Sinuhe on his flight into Syria-Palestine.

Manetho. Egyptian priest who lived during the third century B.C. in the Ptolemaic Period. He wrote a now lost *History of Egypt* and is responsible for organizing the Egyptian kings into dynasties.

Medjai. People from a land to the south, in Nubia. Also at times a professional term: auxiliary troops, policemen, or hunters.

Memphis. The greatest of ancient Egyptian cities, along with Thebes to the south. It stretches for miles across the Nile from modern Cairo and was the administrative center for the government. Its two great burial fields are Giza and Saqqara.

Menna. Historical personage from Deir el-Médineh during the Ramesside period and author of a literary letter to his son, Pay-iry.

Merikare, King. King during Dynasty X (perhaps mid-twenty-first century B.C.) at Heracleopolis. Recipient of the instruction apparently written by King Khety.

Middle Kingdom. See appendix B, "Chronology."

Mighty Goddess, the. Variant of the Great Goddess—possibly Sakhmet.

Min. God of sexual procreativity, usually represented as ithyphallic.

Mistress of the Underworld. Isis?

Mistress of Us All. Epithet of the queen.

Montu. War god of the Theban area, prominent in Dynasty XI and gradually replaced by Amun. Called "Lord of Battle" in *The Tale of Sinuhe.*

Most Holy of Places. Name for the Temple of Karnak in Thebes, domain of Amun.

Name. An essential part of a person. To know someone's name is to have power over that person or deity for good or ill.

Necropolis. Literally, "city of the dead"; the cemetery or burial ground. In ancient Egypt the necropolis was indeed as elaborate as a city, with streets, house-like tombs, a flurry of activity by priests performing the daily rituals at the tombs, and family members arriving to visit the dead, especially on festival days. The most famous of these were at Giza, Saqqara, and Thebes. See also **Place of Truth.**

Neferbau. A deity mentioned in Sinuhe's letter to Senusert I.

Nefertari, Queen. Great Royal Wife of Ramesses II.

Nefertem. God of the lotus; son of Ptah and Sakhmet.

Neferu, Queen. Daughter of Amenemhat I (1991–1962 B.C.) of Dynasty XII and Great Royal Wife of Senusert I (1971–1926 B.C.). Patroness of Sinuhe.

Nepri. The god of grain. He becomes assimilated into the figure of Osiris.

New Kingdom. See appendix B, "Chronology."

Nile River. From its headwaters in Lake Victoria, and with a length of about 3,400 miles, the Nile provides the water and silt that make life possible in Egypt. As Herodotus said, "Egypt is the gift of the Nile."

Nile Valley. Strictly, Upper Egypt. The portion of Egypt that over the eons has cut into the bedrock of northeastern Africa to form a river valley between bluffs or cliffs.

Nine Great Gods. See the **Ennead.**

Nomen. The last of the five names in the royal titulary, emphasizing the king as "Son of the Sun God, Re." This is the name by which Egyptian pharaohs are familiarly known.

Nomes. Term for the districts or "counties" into which ancient Egypt was divided. They probably in some manner reflected the original area of prehistoric settlement. There were twenty-two nomes in Upper Egypt and twenty in Lower Egypt, each with its distinctive emblem and cult center.

North Wind. A cool breeze bringing refreshment to living and dead alike. Since the Nile flows north, the north wind aids the ships sailing south against the current.

Nubians. Peoples to the south of Egypt.

Nun. Designation for the original swirling, windy, and dark watery chaos preceding creation.

Nut. The sky goddess, wife of Geb, the earth.

Old Egyptian. The earliest known stage of the Egyptian language, Dynasties I–VIII (from about the thirty-second century to ca. 2240 B.C.). It is the language of the Pyramid Texts and of the inscriptions of Old Kingdom tombs.

Old Kingdom. See appendix B, "Chronology."

Orion. The constellation seen as an ancient star god who not only strides across the sky but, disappearing at dawn, is resurrected each night. He can confer status on the newly deceased king (as with Ounas) by proclaiming him "one of the Great Ones."

Osiris. One of the greatest gods of ancient Egypt. Son of Geb (earth) and Nut (sky), he represents both the ideal of the good king and the grain, which dies and is reborn. The legend of his marriage to his sister, Isis, his murder by his brother, Seth, the subsequent birth of his son, Horus, and the awarding of the rule of Egypt to Horus by the divine tribunal of the Ennead sitting in judgment between him and Seth—all these form what is perhaps the richest and most complex myth to survive from that culture. He becomes the god of resurrection; and his example demonstrates that one can overcome death and enter into a happy afterlife.

Ostraca. (sing., **ostracon**). Pieces of smoothed limestone or bits of pottery with writing or drawing on them.

Ounas (Unis), King. Last king of Dynasty V. Reigned 2340–2320 B.C. On the walls of his burial chamber are carved the first version of the earliest major body of religious texts in the world, the Pyramid Texts. They comprise spells, sayings, hymns, and other material designed to aid in the resurrection of the dead king.

Our Great Lady. Perhaps an epithet of Sakhmet, especially as the one who causes and removes the plague. Possibly a mother-goddess.

Papyrus (pl., **papyri**). Strips were cut from the stem of the papyrus plant, flattened, and glued together into sheets. This became the writing surface used throughout ancient Egyptian history. Significant also in relation to Lower Egypt, known as the "Land of Papyri."

Pay-iry. Troublesome son in "Menna's Lament."

Peten. Unknown locale in the Great Salt Sea marshes of the eastern Delta.

Philae. Island in the Nile just south of modern Aswan. Site of a major temple of Isis and one of the last places celebrating the ancient religion.

Place of Truth. Designation for the necropolis, especially that of Western Thebes. All the men of Deir el-Medineh worked in the Place of Truth. See also **Necropolis.**

Pomegranate nome. The district of Middle Egypt in the Fayyum; its major center was Heracleopolis.

Pope, Alexander (1688–1744). British poet.

Pound, Ezra (1885–1972). American expatriate poet.

Pot marks. Scratched or incised markings on the surfaces of pottery (or other material) of the Thinite period (Dynasties I–II). Most of the signs are undeciphered, but they are sometimes accompanied by royal names.

Prayers. Ancient Egyptian poems similar to the hymns but requesting something of a deity rather than simply offering homage.

Prenomen. The fourth of the five royal names, emphasizing the king's rule over a united Egypt as "He who belongs to the Sedge [of Upper Egypt] and the Bee [of Lower Egypt]." Like the nomen, it is enclosed in a cartouche.

Prosody. The aspect of stylistics or poetics that deals specifically with versification, that is, with the rhythms or meters of poems.

Ptah. The creator god of Memphis. Husband to Sakhmet and father of Nefertem. He created the universe by thinking it and speaking out the names of its parts.

Ptahhotep. Old kingdom sage, vizier to King Izezi (2380–2340 B.C.) of Dynasty V, and author of the *Maxims*, the oldest didactic text to survive complete from ancient Egypt.

Punt. Country down the Red Sea coast in eastern Africa. Source of tropical goods and exotic merchandise.

Pyramid. At first, the burial place only of pharaohs (and sometimes their immediate family). Seen by the Egyptians as the earthly dwelling of the god-on-earth who had now gone to his true home with the other gods. The royal pyramid tradition continued from late Dynasty III (Djoser) through the Middle Kingdom. There are about forty of them. In the New Kingdom the nobles would often have a small pyramid of their own attached to their tombs.

Pyramid Texts. The body of religious spells, sayings, hymns, and other material carved into the royal tomb of Ounas (Dynasty V) and the kings (and some queens) of Dynasty VI to aid them in their journey to the next world, the realm of the gods where they properly belong.

Qa-nefer. Name either of the mortuary temple or of the pyramid complex (or "city") of Amenemhat I, Queen Neferu's father.

Qedem. Locale in Syria-Palestine visited by Sinuhe.

Queen of Heaven. Epithet applied to various goddesses, perhaps the sky goddess Nut in *The Tale of Sinuhe*. The identity of the various goddesses referred to in the Song of the Princesses in *Sinuhe* is not clear.

Quiet man, the. Designation for the ideal man in the Egyptian instructional or didactic tradition. The concept cannot be translated by a single word. The man who is "quiet" actually is reflective, judicious, unassuming, even-tempered, self-sufficient, and self-effacing, as well as intelligent and eloquent.

Ramesses II, King. Third king of Dynasty XIX. Reigned 1290–1224 B.C. Inveterate builder and husband of Queen Nefertari.

Ramesside Period. The latter portion of the New Kingdom, comprising Dynasties XIX–XX (1305–1080 B.C.). So called for the eleven kings named "Ramesses."

Re. The great creator god and sun god of Heliopolis.

Red Crown. The royal crown representing dominion over Lower Egypt. Sometimes personified as a goddess.

Rensi. The Lord High Steward to King Khety III Nebkaure of Dynasty X (twenty-first century B.C.) who listens to the complaints of the Eloquent Peasant.

Residence, the. Usual designation for the royal capital.

River, the. Always the Nile, the only actual river in Egypt.

Royal Friend. An honorific title given by a king to specially favored courtiers, like Sinuhe.

Sakhmet. "The Powerful One." The lioness goddess of Memphis, daughter of Re and wife of Ptah. She is goddess of war, sickness, plague, and destruction.

Saqqara (Sakkara). Along with Giza, the main burial ground for Memphis. One of the greatest archaeological sites in the world, particularly rich in tombs of the Thinite and Old Kingdom periods.

Scribe. The ancient Egyptian writer, usually a professional bureaucrat or lower-level official. But the scribal schools, like that at Deir el-Medineh, are famous for teaching the young their letters and introducing them to the classic literature of ancient Egypt.

Sedge. The reed-like plant used as an emblem of Upper Egypt. See also **He of the Sedge and the Bee.**

Sehetep-ib-re, King. The prenomen of King Amenemhat I (1991–1962 B.C.), first king of Dynasty XII.

Seizer of Scalp-locks; He of the Upreared Head; Chief over Blood Rites; Traveler; the Bloody-Eyed. All names of minor deities in the other world who hunt down, kill, and process the bodies of the enemies of King Ounas.

Semseru. A deity allied to Sopdu.

Senmut. Fort at the First Cataract of the Nile in the south of Egypt near modern Aswan.

Senusert I, King. Second King of Dynasty XII. Reigned 1971–1926 B.C.

Serpent, the. The royal uraeus on the king's brow and a goddess whose function was to protect the king from his enemies. Also known as the "Eye of Re."

Seth. The great antagonist god in the Osirian legends, brother (and murderer) of Osiris, uncle of Horus, whose kingdom he tried to usurp. He is also the mythological embodiment of bad character, brute strength, and disruptiveness. Actually, the figure of Seth is more complex than this; and as god of the sterile deserts or in other legends, he is the equal, helper, and companion of Horus.

Shu. The god of air in the Heliopolitan theogony, son of Atum (or Re) and consort of Tefnut, the moisture.

Sinuhe. Title character of one of the finest literary pieces to survive from ancient Egypt. His tale is presented as if it were a tomb biography of a courtier living in Dynasty XII during the reigns of Amenemhat I and Senusert I. In the account he is depicted as an intimate in the retinue of Queen Neferu and her children, but no historical evidence for the existence of Sinuhe has yet come to light.

Sistrum (pl. sistra). A hand-held rattle-like percussion instrument. The nearest modern equivalents are the castanet and the tambourine.

Skyship. See **Barque of Re.**

Sneferu's Island. A locale in Egypt, presumably near Sneferu's pyramid, along Sinuhe's flight into exile in Syria-Palestine.

Sobek. Crocodile god connected with royal power and particularly worshipped in the Fayyum. Son of Neith.

Sobek-Re. Fusion of the god Sobek with the power and concept of the more venerable god Re.

Son of the Northwind. Teasing mispronunciation (*Sa-mehyt*) of Sinuhe's name by the royal princesses. See next entry.

Son of the Sycamore. Literal translation of Sinuhe's name (*Sa-nehet*).

Sopdu. Star god and lord of the eastern deserts and the turquoise mines in Sinai.

Spell. To us, a "magical" saying; but to the Egyptians a recitation that invoked supernatural power in order to accomplish some desired human purpose.

Sphinx. Royal figure with the head of a king and the body of a lion, betokening royal power. The most famous Sphinx lies at Giza in front of the pyramid of King Khaefre (2540–2515 B.C., Dynasty IV) and represents his figure. The Egyptian sphinx is not to be confused with the Greek sphinx, an enigmatic female monster featured in Greek mythology and literature.

Staircase of Fire. In the otherworld, presumably the stairway leading up to the presence of Re.

Stela. (p. **stelae**): A stone or slab, set upright and inscribed and/or carved to commemorate a person (i.e., a gravestone) or an event, such as a military victory (a historical stela).

Strabo. First-century B.C. Greek historian and geographer. Egypt is discussed in the final book of his *Geography*.

Sumero-Akkadian literature. Collective term for the literature of the first civilizations of the Tigris-Euphrates river valley: Sumer, on present evidence the earliest known literate civilization anywhere (end of the fourth millennium B.C.), and Akkad, which challenged and succeeded it.

Sunfolk. Term for the blessed dead as they are conceived as traveling with the sun in its journey across the heavens. A concept from the sky religion of Re as opposed to the earth religion centering on Osiris.

Sycamore. The fig tree prized for its shade but also seen as a tree-goddess, perhaps Hathor, sometimes Nut. Sinuhe is "Son of the Sycamore," but his name might be translated "Son belonging to the Sycamore-goddess."

Syria-Palestine. Common collective name for the lands of the eastern Mediterranean now comprising Syria, Lebanon, and Israel.

Taiyt. Goddess of weaving, especially of the cloth for embalming.

Tales. One of the major genres of ancient Egyptian literature. The modern term would be "fiction." The tales range from the very unassuming to the highly sophisticated. Closely associated in form with the tale is myth.

Ta-tenen. "Land rising." The god who represents the emergence of the fertilized land from the waters of the inundation or the first hill of creation from the original chaos. Located at Memphis, he was assimilated into Ptah.

Tefnut. The goddess of moisture, in the Heliopolitan cosmogony, daughter of the creator god and consort of Shu.

Thebes. The greatest city in ancient Egypt, but perhaps sharing that honor with Memphis. Religious capital of Egypt, possibly from the Middle Kingdom on but certainly so during the New Kingdom and later. Not to be confused with the Greek Thebes of the Oedipus story.

Thomas, Dylan (1914–1953). British (Welsh) poet.

Thoth. The god of wisdom, writing, the sacred books, scribes, and intellectual and literary achievement in general.

Thought couplets. The structuring device of most ancient Egyptian poetry. The verse lines occur in pairs, each line composed of (usually) one clause, either dependent or independent, and the pair making up the full sentence and the complete thought.

Titulary (Royal). Term for the formal series of five great names for the Egyptian pharaoh, consisting of (1) the Horus name, symbolizing the king's relationship to the cosmic falcon god; (2) the Two Ladies name (*nebty*) expressing his connection with the two most important goddesses of Upper and Lower Egypt at the beginning of Dynasty I, the vulture-goddess Nekhbet and the cobra-goddess Edjo, respectively; (3) the Horus of Gold name, the significance of which is not clear; (4) the prenomen (*n-sw-bity*; "He of the Sedge and the Bee"), which expresses his relationship to the symbolic plant of Upper Egypt and the symbolic animal of Lower Egypt; and (5) the nomen ("Son of Re"), which signifies his kinship with the sun god. It is the last two of these that are most common and are enclosed in cartouches.

Tutankhamun, King. Reigned 1346–1336 B.C. The boy-king whose mummy and virtually intact funerary treasure were discovered in 1922 by Howard Carter, just one century after Champollion deciphered the hieroglyphs.

Twin Lands. See **Two Lands.**

Two Ladies. The second, or *nebty*, name in the royal titulary, signifying the king's rule of the united Two Lands under the symbols of their tutelary goddesses: Nekhbet, the vulture-goddess of Upper Egypt, and Wadjet, the snake-goddess of Lower Egypt.

Two Lands. A common name for Egypt as the union of two originally separate lands.

Two Phoenicians coastlands. In *The Tale of Sinuhe*, term for the lands of the *Fenekhu* as of the twentieth century B.C. and presumably the ancestors of those who became known to history as the Phoenicians.

Two Shores. Another common name for Egypt, emphasizing the eastern and western banks of the Nile.

Underworld. The place of the afterlife according to ancient Egyptian religion. For all who passed the Final Judgment by Osiris, it meant a life of happiness, fulfillment, and ease, eternally in the presence of God.

Upper Egypt. Southern Egypt, the river valley.

Upper Retenu. Locale in Syria-Palestine where Sinuhe spent most of his life in exile. Ruled by Prince Amunenshi and containing the district of Yaa, the land given to Sinuhe by the prince.

Uraeus (pl., **uraei**). See **The Serpent.**

Ur-waters. The original or primordial watery waste before creation of the universe.

Valley of the Kings. The royal necropolis in Western Thebes during the New Kingdom.

Vizier. The highest official in the Egyptian state under the king. He was charged with the upholding of justice and had complete control over all the country's administrative machinery.

Walls-of-the-Ruler. A fort at the northeastern border of Egypt, built by Amenemhat I of Dynasty XII to fend off and control Asiatic nomads. Sinuhe passes it in his flight to Syria-Palestine.

Wawat. The northernmost region of Nubia at the border with Egypt.

West, the. Symbolic name for the region of the dead. To go to the West means to die. The idea included the final crossing of the Nile to the burial ground on the west bank. It also meant a happy and vigorous afterlife.

White Crown. The crown of Upper Egypt, sometimes personified as a goddess.

Whitman, Walt (1819–1892). American poet.

Wisdom texts. A common name for a variety of didactic or admonitory literary works intended to pass on one's wisdom and experience to the next generation.

Word of God. The sacred writings of ancient Egypt written in the sacred language (the hieroglyphs or hieratic). They were not canonized into a single scripture but recorded those moments when a god spoke to human beings.

Yaa. The district of Upper Retenu given to Sinuhe as a wedding gift by Amunenshi.

Yahwist, the. The earliest writer whose hand is visible in composition of the Pentateuch. A southerner (Judean) who perhaps lived at court during the United Monarchy and wrote circa 950 B.C.

Select Bibliography

Aldred, Cyril. *Akhenaten: King of Egypt*. London: Thames and Hudson, 1988.

Aldred, Cyril. *Egyptian Art*. New York: Oxford University Press, 1980.

Aldred, Cyril. *The Egyptians*. rev. ed. London: Thames and Hudson, 1987.

Baines, John, and Jaromír Málek. *Atlas of Ancient Egypt*. New York: Facts on File, 1980.

Bierbrier, Morris. *The Tomb-Builders of the Pharaohs*. London: British Museum, 1982.

Cambridge Ancient History. 3rd. ed., vols. 1 and 2. Cambridge: Cambridge University Press, 1970–75.

David, Rosalie. *The Pyramid Builders of Ancient Egypt*. London: Routledge & Kegan Paul, 1986.

Edwards, Amelia B. *A Thousand Miles Up the Nile*. 1891. Reprint. Los Angeles: J. P. Tarcher, 1983.

Edwards, I. E. S. *The Pyramids of Egypt*. rev. ed. New York: Viking Penguin, 1986.

Emery, W. B. *Archaic Egypt*. Baltimore: Penguin Books, 1961.

Faulkner, R. O. *The Ancient Egyptian Book of the Dead*. rev. ed. New York: Macmillan, 1985.

Foster, John L. *Love Songs of the New Kingdom*. New York: Charles Scribner's Sons, 1974. Reprint. Austin: University of Texas Press, 1992.

Frankfort, H., H. A. Frankfort, J. A. Wilson, and T. Jacobson. *Before Philosophy*. Baltimore: Penguin Books, 1954.

Freed, Rita. *Ramesses the Great: His Life and World*. Memphis, TN: City of Memphis, 1987.

Gardiner, Sir Alan. *Egyptian Grammar*. 3rd ed. Oxford: Griffith Institute, 1957.

Gardiner, Sir Alan. *Egypt of the Pharaohs*. Oxford: Oxford University Press, 1961.

Harris, J. R., ed. *The Legacy of Egypt*. 2nd ed. Oxford: Oxford University Press, 1971.

Hart, George. *A Dictionary of Egyptian Gods and Goddesses*. London: Routledge & Kegan Paul, 1986.

Hornung, Erik. *Conceptions of God in Ancient Egypt: The One and the Many*. Translated by John Baines. Ithaca: Cornell University Press, 1982.

Hornung, Erik. *The Valley of the Kings: Horizon of Eternity*. New York: Timken, 1990.

James, T. G. H. *An Introduction to Ancient Egypt*. New York: Farrar Straus Giroux, 1979.

James, T. G. H. *Pharaoh's People: Scenes from Life in Imperial Egypt*. Chicago: University of Chicago Press, 1984.

Kemp, Barry J. *Ancient Egypt: Anatomy of a Civilization*. London: Routledge & Kegan Paul, 1989.

Kitchen, K. A. *Pharaoh Triumphant: The Life and Times of Ramesses II*. Warminster: Aris & Phillips, 1982.

133

Lange, K., and M. Hirmer. *Egypt: Architecture, Sculpture, Painting.* 5th ed. London: Phaidon, 1978.

Lauer, Jean-Philippe. *Saqqara: The Royal Cemetery of Memphis.* New York: Charles Scribner's Sons, 1976.

Lichtheim, Miriam. *Ancient Egyptian Literature: A Book of Readings.* 3 vols. Berkeley: University of California Press, 1973–76.

Manniche, Lise. *City of the Dead: Thebes in Egypt.* Chicago: University of Chicago Press, 1987.

Martin, Geoffrey T. *The Hidden Tombs of Memphis.* London: Thames and Hudson, 1991.

Mekhitarian, Arpag. *Egyptian Painting.* Geneva: Skira, 1954.

Morenz, Siegfried. *Egyptian Religion.* Translated by Ann E. Keep. London: Methuen, 1973.

Nims, Charles F. *Thebes of the Pharaohs.* New York: Stein and Day, 1965.

Peck, William H., and John G. Ross. *Egyptian Drawings.* New York: E. P. Dutton, 1978.

Posener, Georges. "Literature." Chap. 9 in *The Legacy of Egypt,* edited by J. R. Harris. 2nd ed. Oxford: Oxford University Press, 1971.

Posener, Georges, Serge Sauneron, and Jean Yoyotte. *Dictionary of Egyptian Civilization.* Translated by Alix Macfarlane. New York: Tudor, 1959.

Redford, Donald B. *Akhenaten: The Heretic King.* Princeton: Princeton University Press, 1984.

Riefstahl, Elizabeth. *Thebes in the Time of Amunhotep III.* Norman: University of Oklahoma Press, 1964.

Romano, James F., *Catalogue of the Luxor Museum of Ancient Egyptian Art.* Cairo: American Research Center in Egypt, 1979.

Russman, Edna R. *Egyptian Sculpture: Cairo and Luxor.* Austin: University of Texas Press, 1989.

Simpson, W. K., R. O. Faulkner, and E. F. Wente. *The Literature of Ancient Egypt.* rev. ed. New Haven: Yale University Press, 1973.

Smith, W. Stevenson. *The Art and Architecture of Ancient Egypt.* Revised by W. K. Simpson. Harmondsworth: Penguin Books, 1958, 1981.

Trigger, B. G., B. J. Kemp, D. O'Connor, and A. B. Lloyd. *Ancient Egypt: A Social History.* Cambridge: Cambridge University Press, 1983.

Wilson, John A. *The Culture of Ancient Egypt.* Chicago: University of Chicago Press, 1956. Originally published as *The Burden of Egypt,* 1951.

Yoyotte, Jean. *Treasures of the Pharaohs.* Geneva: Skira, 1968.